TO

FROM

DATE

single and not sorry

90 DEVOTIONS OF REAL ENCOURAGEMENT FOR RIGHT NOW

DaySpring
LIVE YOUR FAITH

CONTENTS

HEY READER,

Thank you for picking up this book. As a fellow single woman, it's my hope that these devotions will encourage your heart, refresh your spirit, and remind you that you, too, can be single and not sorry. From personal experience, I know that singleness is full of ups and downs. My goal in writing this book was to remind you again and again that, although you are single, you are never alone. God is always with you. Not only that, but you have an amazing community of other singles ready to prove that to you.

You are valuable because of who God created you to be, not because of your relationship status. As you read this devotional, each day will end with a "right now reminder." This is meant to affirm you and remind you that the season you are in right now is beautiful and full in its own ways. You are not missing out, and you are not behind.

Single and Not Sorry is a call for us to be all we can be in Jesus. We can be bold, confident, and free. We don't need a relationship to affirm what God is stirring up in our hearts and calling us to. May the following pages remind you that you are whole and powerful just as you are.

We got this!

Ellen

Ellen Wildman

CONNECT WITH ME ON INSTAGRAM
@ELLEN_WILDMAN OR ON ELLENWILDMAN.COM.

EMERGENCY CONTACTS

*Just as our bodies have many parts and each part
has a special function, so it is with Christ's body.
We are many parts of one body,
and we all belong to each other.*
ROMANS 12:4–5 NLT

We all need an emergency contact: at the doctor, at work, even when booking a vacation. As single women, this simple box that appears over and over again on informational forms can tug at our anxiety and reignite our sadness over our relationship status. If we aren't in the right headspace, it can remind us that we aren't coupled up and that we don't have a built-in, go-to person. But just because we don't have an obvious emergency contact does not mean we're alone. Far from it! As Romans tells us, we are an essential part of the body of Christ. It doesn't mention our relationship status or our dating mishaps. God opens up opportunities for relationships with friends who feel like brothers and sisters who are deeply invested in our lives.

We all have a support network: at church, in our various friend groups, and with our family. If we dedicate ourselves to this community, investing our time and energy in relationships, a deep bond of brotherhood and sisterhood will emerge. As these verses show, God's plan is for us to be united with others. When we get sick and need help, it only feels natural to call up one of our friends. When we're stressed and need to talk through an issue, we have understanding friends and family on speed dial. When we need an emergency contact, it's a matter of which person to choose, not of racking our brain for a willing body. This deep and trusting community will take time, but God knows the desires of your heart. His plan for you is to be an essential member of the body. He has created you as a part of a community that cares for and loves one another, no ring required.

RIGHT NOW REMINDER:

You are loved by so many, and you are part of a beautiful community that cares for you. We belong to one another.

YOU ARE NOT BEHIND

Many are the plans in the mind of a man,
but it is the purpose of the LORD that will stand.
PROVERBS 19:21 ESV

As kids, we plan and dream about how our lives will unfold. Maybe you envisioned a life that looked different than it does right now. Perhaps you dreamed about walking down the aisle in a white gown to meet your one true love at the altar. Maybe you assumed you would get married right out of college, or you were in a relationship that you thought would last forever. It's possible that your five-year plan included marriage or your ten-year plan included kids. But here you are, single, whether by choice or by circumstance. As you attend engagement parties, weddings, and baby shower after baby shower, it can be difficult not to turn inward and feel like you are falling behind. But those lies—the ones that say you are behind everyone else, that you are doing something wrong because you aren't in a relationship—are not from the Lord. He says you are right where you're meant to be.

Our God is a God of goodness. He planned out your life as an overflow of this goodness. While you may have had a vision for your life that looked different, you can trust that God knows what He's doing. Think back on a time when you clearly felt the Lord's leading. Maybe it was a job change that you'd been hoping for, an unexpected move that turned out to be the perfect thing for you, or another obvious and direct answer to prayer. That same leading is working in you now, directing your path as the Lord's purposes are displayed through you. It's natural to question your life when it looks different from many friends and family around you, but know that God hasn't questioned His plan or your relationship status for a second. He knows exactly what He's doing, and He isn't afraid. It's not wrong to plan and to dream. Let the Lord know your desires, and let His peace fill you as you remember the goodness of His plan. You are not behind, and you never have been. You are right where you need to be.

RIGHT NOW REMINDER:

God's plan for your relationship status and your life isn't off course. His goodness is on display in you right now, right where you are.

THE GOODNESS OF TIME

*So be careful how you act; these are difficult days.
Don't be fools; be wise: make the most of
every opportunity you have for doing good.*
EPHESIANS 5:15–16 TLB

We are all busy. Maybe you're a student, rushing from class to work to the library with barely a minute to down some coffee. Maybe you work a demanding full-time job and balance a busy side hustle after hours. Maybe you're really involved in your local community, and it's rare for you to have a night where you aren't out and about. We all feel like we're short on time. But believe it or not, one of the great gifts of singleness is the flexibility of this precious resource.

Sure, we can fill up our calendars just as quickly as those in a relationship or with kids. The difference is, we get to choose to say yes or no to something after simply weighing our own options, instead of comparing multiple color-coordinated calendars or penciling in lunch with a friend between a kid's soccer practice and that potluck. We are in control of our time in a unique way, and we can often decide if we want to do something or not based solely on our own desires. Ephesians advises us to "make the most of every opportunity you have for doing good." As single women, we are uniquely positioned to do just that.

God has placed you in this season for a reason, and His desire for you is that you would do good with your flexible timetable—whether your singleness lasts a week, a year, or a lifetime. So what would it look like to utilize some of your time for the goodness of God? What activity stirs your heart and gets you excited to do good? It could be volunteering a few hours a week at your local homeless shelter, offering to babysit for a family at your church, or cooking a meal for your friends who are having a hard week. Doing good doesn't have to be a grand production or take up every hour of your day. But since you are gifted with the flexibility of time, why not pencil in a few hours for serving someone else?

RIGHT NOW REMINDER:

God wants to meet you right where you are
and do great things through you.
You can use your time to spread His love.

SINGLENESS IS A GIFT

I wish that all people were as I am.
But each has his own gift from God,
one person has this gift, another has that.

I CORINTHIANS 7:7 CSB

The apostle Paul, one of the heroes of the Christian faith and the author of thirteen New Testament books, was just as single as you and I. He penned letters of his miraculous testimony—how he went from being a persecutor of Christians to preacher of the gospel. In today's verse, we see that Paul actually told the church in Corinth that singleness was a gift. As a matter of fact, he wishes that more people were single like him! For many of us, the idea that singleness is a gift feels radical and uneasy. You might long for a relationship, for marriage and a family, and that's okay. Your singleness can still be a gift while you simultaneously pray to exchange this gift for marriage in the future. While you are single, however, there is celebration to be found.

Paul writes later in I Corinthians 7 that one of the benefits of this gift is that we can be focused on the Lord (see v. 35). What if we use this season of singleness to narrow our focus, connecting more with God and deepening our relationship with Him? The gift of singleness provides us with mental and emotional capacity to commit our hearts in prayer, worship, and time spent with God. What if we reframe our days and our activities as opportunities to spend time with Him? Reframing singleness as a gift ultimately brings us closer to the Gift Giver and helps us focus on the beauty of this season, no matter how long it lasts.

RIGHT NOW REMINDER:

Your singleness is a gift.
Part of this gift is the opportunity to
focus more on your relationship with the Lord.
He loves you so much, and He is ready
and waiting to connect with you.

RELATIONSHIP STATUS

Trust in the Lord with all your heart;
do not depend on your own understanding.
Seek His will in all you do,
and He will show you which path to take.
PROVERBS 3:5–6 NLT

If you've been single for any length of time, you've likely been bombarded with questions like "How's dating going?" "Anyone new you've been seeing?" or, the straight to the point, "Do you have a new boyfriend?" While friends and family that ask these types of questions are usually well-meaning, depending on how you're feeling about your relationship status, it can be awkward, frustrating, and disappointing to navigate this type of small talk. When these conversations arise, it's helpful to remember that sometimes other people just don't know what else to ask. For many, a dating or marriage relationship is the biggest thing that can happen in life. Maybe your priorities are different, maybe you feel called to invest elsewhere right now, or maybe it simply bums you out to be asked about your relationship status on a near daily basis. Well, in case you haven't heard in a while, you are so much more than your relationship status.

God doesn't look at you and see a single person in need of a partner. Far from it! He sees you as His beloved daughter, created by Him and loved just as you are. In fact, it isn't as if God has to overlook your relationship status in order to accept you. He doesn't consider your singleness a negative in any way because He planned out your life this way! Your passions, your purpose, and, yes, your singleness are all a part of His perfect plan for this one wild and crazy life. Even if others don't understand your feelings about singleness, even if you don't understand why you've found yourself in this season, you can trust the Lord as He guides you through it. He will never let you down. And next time your aunt asks about your dating status, remind yourself that you are on the path God has laid out for you, and it is good. You don't need to understand His plan to trust that it will be beautiful.

RIGHT NOW REMINDER:

*Your relationship status
does not determine your worth.
Never has, never will.*

GOD DOESN'T CONSIDER YOUR SINGLENESS A NEGATIVE IN ANY WAY, BECAUSE HE PLANNED YOUR LIFE OUT THIS WAY! YOUR PASSIONS, YOUR PURPOSE, AND, YES, YOUR SINGLENESS ARE ALL A PART OF HIS PERFECT PLAN FOR THIS ONE WILD AND CRAZY LIFE.

GIFTED GLORY-BRINGERS

God has given each of you a gift from His great variety
of spiritual gifts. Use them well to serve one another.
Do you have the gift of speaking? Then speak as though
God Himself were speaking through you. Do you have
the gift of helping others? Do it with all the strength and
energy that God supplies. Then everything you do
will bring glory to God through Jesus Christ.
All glory and power to Him forever and ever! Amen.

I PETER 4:10–11 NLT

Every person you know—friend, family member, and even stranger—has a unique and beautiful gift. Maybe you have a friend whose empathy ushers healing into the lives of many, while another expresses her creativity in fresh and stunning ways. Maybe a family member volunteers their time to help others or opens their home to the hurting in their community. We are each gifted uniquely to show God's love through different avenues, and others are gifted in ways we are not. As Peter tells us in today's verses, we are each given a spiritual gift from God. It cannot be denied: you have been given a gift by God.

Notice also that this passage says nothing about one's marital status. It can be tempting to withhold the greatest parts of yourself for later—for a relationship, for marriage, for someday. But God has given you the strength and energy to exercise your gift right now. You can be a light to the world because of who you are in this moment, not waiting until the elusive "someday." Through the exercising of your gift, you are bringing glory to God, and what could be better than that? The opportunity to be a glory-bringer certainly cannot wait for a walk down the aisle. Perhaps you're gifted in speaking or teaching, cooking or crafting, in generosity or in peacemaking. Powered by God, you can live out your gifts today. The world needs you, glory-bringer, and it needs you today.

RIGHT NOW REMINDER:

You have a God-given gift that you can use to serve others. Don't wait to exercise it. The world needs everything you have to offer right now.

ALWAYS SUPPORTED

Carry one another's burdens;
in this way you will fulfill the law of Christ.
GALATIANS 6:2 CSB

For many of us, getting sick is a painful reminder of our relationship status. Even if you are at a place where you are content with your singleness, when you're sick, all you want is for someone to be there to make you some healing soup, run out and get you medicine, and bring you a glass of orange juice as you melt into the couch. Whether you live on your own, with a roommate, or with family, sickness can become a time when your walls are down, and you are susceptible to the track of lies that plays in the back of your mind. Lies such as "no one cares for you" and "you have to do it all on your own" may echo in your head as you curl up in bed, feeling even more miserable than before. That is, until you start taking others up on the offer to help. You see, your friends and family want to help to heal you, but you have to say yes. It can be humbling to admit, especially for us single women who pride ourselves on being independent, that sometimes we do indeed need help. But as soon as you acknowledge to yourself and to others that you need them, your loneliness will vanish, and you'll feel the love and support you need as your body heals.

In Galatians, Paul calls Christians to carry one another's burdens. Just as we desire to help others in need, our brothers and sisters in Christ desire to do the same for us! All we have to do is ask for help. It can be difficult, but if you put aside your pride and ask others for help, you'll be blessed by each person who is ready to rally around you. Just because you're single doesn't mean you have or need to go through tough times alone. Ask for help when you need it so the body of Christ can be there for you.

RIGHT NOW REMINDER:

Whether you're sick or just having a rough week, ask those around you for help when you need it. Oftentimes others are waiting for an opportunity to show you God's love in a tangible way.

UJING THIJ TIME

Grow in grace and understanding
of our Master and Savior, Jesus Christ.
Glory to the Master, now and forever! Yes!
II PETER 3:18 THE MESSAGE

Chances are at some point during your singleness, someone will advise you to use this time to prepare for marriage. And while singleness is a great time to get to know yourself better, to deepen your relationship with God, and to grow your community, you do not need to actively try to get ready to be a great and godly wife when you don't even have a boyfriend. There are so many beautiful benefits of this time in your life, and you squander them when you are focused on the future or fixated on being a great wife to a good husband. You can invest in yourself, heal your heart, and grow in God, all while enjoying your singleness for the gift that it is. You do not need to use this time to prepare for something you aren't necessarily promised. This notion, that as singles we are preparing for something far better and more lovely than our life now, robs us of our joy today and perpetuates the idea that married couples have reached a higher level of maturity or have figured out their life more. And when you try to skip ahead of the season you're in now, you miss all the goodness and glory in the here and now.

If you have received advice to prepare for marriage, it's important to remember that marriage is different but not better. Just as singleness comes with its inherent set of challenges, struggles, and blessings, so too does marriage. One does not simply become more mature or more spiritual when they exchange rings and sign the marriage license. So use this time however you feel God is calling you to, but release yourself from the pressure of your single life acting as a staging area from when your married life begins. Grow toward Christ, not toward marriage.

RIGHT NOW REMINDER:

Release yourself from any pressure of using this time as a single woman to prepare for marriage. Instead of focusing on growing toward marriage, grow toward Christ.

GENEROSITY OF HEART

Give, and it will be given to you.
Good measure, pressed down, shaken together,
running over, will be put into your lap. For with the
measure you use it will be measured back to you.
LUKE 6:38 ESV

As a single woman, chances are you don't have a KitchenAid mixer from a wedding shower or a nice set of sheets from a bridal brunch. You've probably never received cutlery as a gift or a box of monogrammed towels at your doorstep. Especially as a single woman who may have to bear the burden of expenses that would otherwise be shared, being a good steward of your money is important. Consequently, most of us worry about money and feel as though we don't have enough, always evaluating what we can purchase and if we can go to this event or that dinner. So it seems counterintuitive that by giving away some of our hard-earned money, we will actually become richer. Perhaps our riches aren't measured in dollars and cents but in something greater. Perhaps we can use our money to change others' lives and to spread the gospel.

Budgets, savings goals, and emergency funds are all important. Generosity of heart doesn't overlook these legitimate plans. Instead, generosity of heart looks to give in ways big and small to help those around you. The Bible shows us over and over examples of those who had only a little to give to God, but because they gave it with a humble attitude and a loving spirit, they were rewarded (see Mark 12:41–44, Luke 19:11–27). You are single and you may have limited resources, but that doesn't mean you can't be generous. Being generous with the little you have will shake up your pride, calm your anxiety over your finances, and provide you with the peace of knowing that God has always been in control. The amazing thing is, once you become more charitable with your money, you will experience a freedom over your capital that only generosity can bring. Ask God where and how you can give of your time and money, and He will lead you to this freedom.

RIGHT NOW REMINDER:

Ask the Lord what generosity looks like for you right now.
He is faithful to provide for you and is ready
to work through you to bless others.

FIVE-YEAR PLANS

The heart of man plans his way,
but the LORD establishes his steps.
PROVERBS 16:9 ESV

"Where do you see yourself in five years?" No matter your age or life stage, you've probably heard this question quite a few times. Especially as single women, it can be difficult to map out a five-year plan that doesn't feel like you are expecting too much or too little but also takes your desires and dreams into account. As today's verse in Proverbs tells us, the Lord will establish our steps and make clear His plan for our life. Not only is this a good plan, it is a glorious and beautiful life that is far beyond what you could ask or imagine (see Ephesians 3:20). Here's what it comes down to: it's okay for you to be a little fuzzy on your ideal plan for your life because the Lord's vision for you is crystal clear. Isn't it exciting that you are along for the journey?

When looking into your future, you will experience the most peace when you trust your unknown future to a known God. We know that God loves us more than we can even fathom, and we know that He has mapped out our lives with love and care. Instead of worrying about what this next year, five years, or ten years could look like, why not reframe it to see that God has you on an adventure that is all your own? Isn't it exciting to see the unveiling of what He has planned for you? The next time someone asks you about your five-year plan, don't be afraid to dream. God knows no boundaries, and He is with you, so there's nothing out of the realm of possibilities.

RIGHT NOW REMINDER:

God has BIG plans for you
so don't be afraid to dream.
You don't have to figure out
how He is going to do it,
just trust Him in each next step.

YOUR BODY IS NOT A PROBLEM

God created man in His own image;
He created Him in the image of God;
He created them male and female. . . . God saw
all that He had made, and it was very good indeed.
GENESIS 1:27, 31 CSB

When you're absorbed in your feelings about your singleness, it can be tempting to look within to find blame or reason, and it's often natural to turn your focus on your body. Once you hyperfocus on parts of your body that you perceive as flaws or problem areas, you may soon get the idea that changing your body will change your relationship status. Most of us have been there at one time or another. We diet, we push our limits physically, we strive to have that perfect look. The idea that your appearance is linked to your singleness feels logical when you're in this mindset. The truth, however, is not so simple. Your body is not a problem to be solved or an issue to be fixed. The way your body looks does not dictate your relationship status.

Our passage today reminds us that we are

made in the image of God. We know that God is good (see Exodus 34:6), and therefore His creation is good. Your body is not a problem because your body was created by a good God. And not only that, when He created you, He was proud of His creation. If you feel as though your appearance or certain aspects of your body are the reason you are single, remember that you are the *imago Dei*. *Imago Dei* is a Latin term meaning "image of God." that serves as a good reminder that in everything we do, we are image-bearers of God. You are the *imago Dei*.

If anyone has ever told you that they couldn't be with you because of your body, that was not from God. Of course, it is important for us to care for our bodies, but as today's passage explains, our bodies are already good because they were created by Him. Your body is not a problem to be fixed but a beautiful part of God's creation.

RIGHT NOW REMINDER:

You were made in God's image, and your body is good. Your body does not need to be morphed, altered, or changed in any way for you to be loved.

SOUL REST

We all long for some good R&R—rest and relaxation. But did you know that there is a difference between relaxing and resting? Most of the time, relaxing looks something like turning on your favorite sitcom after a long day, scrolling social media while you lounge on the couch, or doing a puzzle while a podcast plays in the background. All of these things can also be restful, but too often we use these activities to redirect our brains, unplug from our lives, and zone out.

In contrast, time spent resting rejuvenates you and tunes you back in to yourself and your needs, re-energizing your soul because it was time spent connecting with your innermost self and with God. Restful activities may look more like sitting on a bench in a park watching the birds, taking a long and much-needed nap over the weekend, or reading your Bible. As a single woman, now is the perfect time to discover what activities give your soul rest. Life will only get busier, and connecting with yourself and God through soul rest now can become a rhythm you carry through all of your days. No matter your relationship status, your soul is always in need of rest.

God has promised to give us rest. We can participate in this promise by finding outlets and activities that fill our souls and draw us back to Him. How can you determine if you've found an outlet for soul rest? Listen to your body. If you feel refreshed, renewed, or re-energized, then that may be the perfect new addition to your self-care toolbox.

RIGHT NOW REMINDER:

God wants to give you rest.
Find an activity (or lack of activity)
this week that fills you up and
makes you feel like yourself again.

SAD BUT SUSTAINED

*Cast your burden upon the L*ORD
and He will sustain you;
He will never allow the righteous to be shaken.

PSALM 55:22 NASB

There will be times in your season of singleness when you just feel sad. Another friend in your friend group gets married, making you the last single woman of the bunch. A coworker makes a hurtful comment like, "But you're so great, I can't imagine why you'd still be single!" A guy you were talking to and getting excited about ghosts you or breaks things off, leaving you with the reminder that you'll have to start all over again. It's not about whether these moments will come, it's more about how you respond when they do. Our passage today reminds us that, especially in these moments of need, you can come to the Lord for strength and sustenance. God is not embarrassed by your feelings, nor is He waiting to exhort you to "cheer up" or "look on the bright side." Whenever you feel sad, He is there for you.

Experiencing ups and downs in your singleness is normal and expected. It's a part of life. It's okay to feel sad, to mourn that your life may not have turned out the way you pictured it. It's okay to cry or to be angry over the loss of a dream. It's also okay to feel frustrated by the well-meaning comments friends and family members make. Whatever you're feeling, it's okay. The important thing to remember is that if you sit in this sadness, nothing will come of it but pain. But if you bring to God the feelings that are weighing you down, He will sustain you. God may not make these feelings go away, but He is a God of life and of peace and is there to offer you both. In times of sadness, He will be that calming presence.

God is with you; He will never leave you. Even in moments of sadness, remember that the Lord is there to support, comfort, and provide for you. He's got you.

RIGHT NOW REMINDER:

*You will experience times of sadness as a single woman.
In these moments, bring your feelings to God,
your sustenance and your peace.*

STICK TO YOUR STANDARDS

Do not be conformed to this age,
but be transformed by the renewing of your mind,
so that you may discern what is the good,
pleasing, and perfect will of God.
ROMANS 12:2 CSB

As kids, most of us were taught to have standards for our significant other. We talk about our "dream guy" with friends, or older ladies ask us, "What exactly are you looking for?" Television shows joke about "deal breakers," and movies remind us that a potential significant other's qualities can be right but not right for us. We spend hours as kids daydreaming about our Prince Charming, imagining a meet-cute where we bump into the ideal guy. The picture's a little fuzzy, but the excitement is there. But fast forward a few years, and you may start questioning that picture, questioning your standards.

If you've been single for a while, you've probably heard something like "Are you sure your standards aren't too high?" or "It seems as though you're looking for the perfect man." Hear this: standards for a significant other are a good, God-given thing. Don't lower your standards because of external pressure or loneliness. Don't settle. Paul tells us in Romans that we should pursue the will of God for our lives, working to dwell in His plan instead of abiding by the standards of success the world dictates. This applies to our standards for our future partner as well. If you know that your boyfriend needs to be a strong Christian, maintain that conviction even when it gets tough. If you believe that your mate needs to be empathetic toward others, don't settle for less. God has given you these standards because He loves you, and He wants to see you flourish in a romantic relationship. He is for you. Align your heart and your standards with God, and feel free to daydream.

RIGHT NOW REMINDER:

You do not need to lower your standards for anyone.
Single while upholding your standards
is better than being in a relationship
because you settled.

HE'S BEEN THERE TOO

Jesus understands every weakness of ours, because He was tempted in every way that we are. But He did not sin! So whenever we are in need, we should come bravely before the throne of our merciful God. There we will be treated with undeserved grace, and we will find help.

HEBREWS 4:15–16 CEV

We can find all sorts of comfort in the fact that Jesus came to earth as a human, facing many of the same hardships, frustrations, and joys that come with the human experience. He got hungry (Mark 11:12), and maybe He even got hangry a time or two. He got tired (John 4:6) and needed to rest and take time away from people. And have you ever thought about how Jesus was single? He not only knows what it's like to be human, He knows what it's like to be single. He understands you even when you feel as though no one else can, because He's been there.

As our passage tells us, the fact that Jesus sees us so well can spur us to come to Him whenever we are in need. As a single woman, you may feel a particular type of need. You may feel lonely and desperate for a reminder that you are not alone. Or maybe you are content in your singleness and are looking to Jesus for affirmation that that's okay, even as those around you question this decision. Perhaps you're unsure about whether you should be looking for a relationship or not. You can come to Him with that too. Jesus knows you so well, and that includes your experience as a single person. You may have had conversations with others about singleness that didn't go so well, leaving you feeling downcast or anxiety ridden, questioning your decisions, or ready to just give up. Not so with Jesus. When you come to Him, He can not only empathize with you but meet you with kindness and help. Jesus understands.

RIGHT NOW REMINDER:

When He came to earth,
Jesus experienced what it was like to be human . . .
including being single. He understands
and empathizes with you.

NO ADVICE NECESSARY

There is one who speaks rashly like the thrusts of a sword,
but the tongue of the wise brings healing.

PROVERBS 12:18 NASB

Not all advice is good advice. As a single woman, you'll receive all sorts of words of encouragement or well-meaning suggestions aimed at your relationship status. But the truth is, some of this advice will be untrue and unhelpful, and you do not need to accept it or agree with it. Even if you respect or admire the one providing you with guidance, you don't have to redirect your heart based on their words. Your singleness, and God's plan for your love life, does not sway to the advice of others.

If you've heard: "God will bring the right person as soon as you stop looking!"

Remember this: Your desire to be in a relationship is not a bad thing. You do not need to tamp it down in order to dwell in God's plan for you and your future relationships. God will bring the right person into your life if and when the time is right.

If you've heard: "You have to love yourself first before someone can love you."

Remember this: While loving yourself and knowing

your worth is extremely important, it is not a precursor for any relationship. God loves you when you don't love yourself, and so do your friends and family.

If you've heard: "You've got to put yourself out there more."

Remember this: You are not obligated to be either in pursuit of or in a relationship at any point in time. It is more important to look inside yourself and determine your desire and where you feel Gods has called you than to force yourself into the dating scene when you aren't interested or ready.

It all comes down to this: You do not have to accept advice that feels discouraging, unhelpful, or makes you feel guilty and weird. While you are single, there will be those who offer rash advice. Surround yourself instead with words that bring healing and life, no matter your relationship status.

RIGHT NOW REMINDER:

*It's okay to reject advice
that doesn't serve you or feel right to you.
Your journey as a single woman is unique,
and no one knows what you need
better than you and God.*

GROUNDED IN GOD

*For God has not given us a spirit of fear and timidity,
but of power, love, and self-discipline.*
II TIMOTHY 1:7 NLT

How does your singleness make you feel? You've likely gone through moments of contentment, angst, frustration, fear, and exasperation . . . maybe all in the same day! Being single in a world that applauds relationships is an emotional undertaking. So maybe the better question is, How does your singleness make you feel *right now*? Maybe you've been burned by a past relationship and are daunted by the idea of dating again. Maybe you've been single for a while and are happy with that, but you're afraid what others will think about your mindset. Maybe you long for a relationship, and the dissatisfaction has left you tired and defeated. Can you imagine if, instead of this storm of emotions, you felt empowered, loved, and confident? This wealth of goodness is what God has called you to. As our verse today shows, you can live a life of singleness—whether for a day, a year, or a lifetime—that overflows with God-given strength.

It's a mindset shift to realize that God has called you to be empowered, self-controlled, and loved. But in a season that is filled to overflowing with emotions, how is this mindset shift attainable? It's all about centering yourself in Him. This could look like prayer, journaling, going for a walk, or listening to worship music. It could mean slowing down and baking, gardening, or creating. Find an activity that fills your soul and makes you feel more connected to God. Just like the uniqueness of singleness, it's okay if your time with Him doesn't look like other people's time with God. You'll notice that as you dwell in His presence and learn more about Him, it's natural for goodness to begin to overflow. By being aware of God's gifts meant for you—such as power, love, and self-discipline—you can reject the lies related to your singleness as they come up. Ground yourself in Him, and even when hard feelings come, you can stand strong.

RIGHT NOW REMINDER:

You will have overwhelming times of sadness and frustration, but God is not a God of fear and of lack, and the more you lean into Him, the more you'll find that you have a solid foundation—one that fills you with all the power, love, and sustenance you need.

ONE DATE AT A TIME

*For there is a time and a way for everything,
although man's trouble lies heavy on him.*
ECCLESIASTES 8:6 ESV

There's a dangerous narrative that is repeated everywhere, from movies to music to the last bridal shower you attended. It goes something like this: "When you know, you know." While sweet, the problem with this message is the accompanying subtle and underlying pressure: when you enter the dating scene and go out with someone, you'll know pretty quickly if you want to marry them or not. It seems like we've lost sight of the reason for dating: to learn about yourself, to meet others, and to help you hone in on what you're looking for in your future mate. The pressure of deciding if you want to spend forever with this person after one cup of coffee or one walk in the park is enough to topple even the most enthusiastic among us. So hear this: whether you are currently dating or deciding whether or not to date, you do not need to decide on your future with someone right away. That's what dating is for, and there is nothing wrong with that.

We've all said (or know someone who's said)

we've met the person we're going to marry . . . and then we didn't. Sometimes this is by choice, sometimes not. But sometimes you think you know, and you just don't. Don't succumb to the unnecessary pressure to make lifelong decisions quickly because that's what you've heard others do. If you are dating, all you have to decide from one date to the next is if you'd like to spend a few more hours with that person. There is a time for everything, including making big decisions in relationships. God will be with you every step of the way, and you don't need to feel any pressure to decide the trajectory of a relationship quickly.

RIGHT NOW REMINDER:

Try not to feel any pressure
to make hasty decisions. God's got you
from one minute to the next.
Rest in that truth today.

BODY REJPECT

*Do you not know that your bodies are
temples of the Holy Spirit, who is in you,
whom you have received from God?
You are not your own; you were bought at a price.
Therefore honor God with your bodies.*

I CORINTHIANS 6:19–20 NIV

What comes to mind when you think of a church? Maybe it's the small-town church you attend weekly, or the busy church with the big white steeple on the corner, or an old stained glass–filled cathedral you toured on vacation. Each of these churches is beautiful in its own way, but we approach them all with respect and care. In this passage in I Corinthians, Paul is instructing us to apply that same reverence and awe to our own bodies. His reasoning here is rooted in the gospel: because Jesus died for our sins on the cross, we were "bought at a price." And if you've accepted God into your heart, His Spirit now dwells within you and alongside you at all times (see Acts 2:38). For these reasons, your body—mind, physical body, and spirit—deserves kindness and respect.

Better still, treating your body with the same

reverence and thoughtfulness that you would a church makes God proud. This body respect could look like speaking more kindly to yourself, working to tune in to your physical needs more (rest when you need it, move when you feel it), or learning more about your own mind through therapy. Respecting your body doesn't look like berating yourself over your singleness, restricting and dieting in order to appear more attractive to others, or changing your likes and dislikes for the sake of another. God's Spirit lives inside you, and He is pleased when you treat all parts of yourself with love. Working to respect your body will teach others to respect you as well.

RIGHT NOW REMINDER:

Your body—
mind, physical body, and spirit—
is worthy of respect and love.

AN IDOL OF THE HEART

Do not have other gods besides me.
Do not make an idol for yourself, whether
in the shape of anything in the heavens above or
on the earth below or in the waters under the earth.
Do not bow in worship to them, and do not serve them;
for I, the LORD your God, am a jealous God, bringing the
consequences of the fathers' iniquity on the children to
the third and fourth generations of those who hate me,
but showing faithful love to a thousand generations of
those who love me and keep my commands.

EXODUS 20:3–6 CSB

In the Old Testament, we find that people worshipped idols (or false gods), like golden statues of animals or idols of crooked kings. But in our day, idols aren't quite so obvious. Instead of a sculpture at the center of town or an ornately decorated replica displayed on an altar, idols of the heart are far more common. These idols of the heart look more like financial success, a large social media following, or a comfortable life. And for single people, the dream of a relationship can also become an idol.

It can be tempting to see friends and family in happy romantic relationships and to place the idea of a relationship on a pedestal or throne in your heart. But the thing is, God is the only one who deserves the throne (see Psalm 103:19). It's okay to desire a relationship and to ask God for that, but it becomes an idol when you treasure, prioritize, or seek fulfillment, comfort, and satisfaction in it over the Lord. Even the idea of a relationship can send the most contented single woman spiraling into idol-centric thinking. Not only does God specifically warn against idols in the Bible, but we know that the idol of relationships will never fulfill you like a relationship with God will. As stated in our passage today, we are called to put Him first. Think about it: are you allowing the idea of a relationship to become an idol? Or are you continuing to make deepening your relationship with God a priority, knowing that it is the most important?

RIGHT NOW REMINDER:

*Ask God to shine His light
on anything you are lifting higher than Him,
and then ask Him to help you re-prioritize.
God is always there for you,
ready to calm you with His faithful love.*

BOASTING IN THE LORD

But the one who boasts is to boast in the Lord.
For it is not the one who commends himself that is
approved, but the one whom the Lord commends.
II CORINTHIANS 10:17–18 NASB

There are benefits to singleness that can't be denied. For most of us, we have complete control over our daily schedules and can come and go as we please. We certainly get more sleep than those who are married and have kids, and we are able to use our money more freely. On the whole, the independence that singleness brings allows us to live a life based solely on our own desires. And while idolizing a relationship can be a struggle for many, being prideful in your singleness is also common. It's okay to enjoy and even prefer being single, but pride comes in when we start to believe that we don't need anyone—including God.

Today's passage reminds us that pride in ourselves will only leave us wanting. The benefits of singleness are real and important, and recognizing them can be a great source of encouragement to those who are struggling with their status as single women. But if we begin to boast in ourselves, thinking we are superior to others because of our singleness, we may begin to believe that we are better off managing our lives on our own. This leaves no room for the Lord, who knows us better than we know ourselves and has planned a better life for us than we could even imagine. Pride blinds us to the work of God in our lives because it makes us focus on ourselves. If we can shift our focus to praising God for the benefits of singleness and looking to Him to be our rock during this season, we will deepen our relationship with Him and boast in His work instead of our own.

RIGHT NOW REMINDER:

Recognizing the benefits of singleness is reassuring, but allowing them to be a source of pride will only hurt you. By praising God for the goodness of this season, your relationship with Him will be strengthened and pride will flee.

PLANS ON PLANS ON PLANS

May the God of hope fill you
with all joy and peace in believing,
so that by the power of the Holy Spirit
you may abound in hope.
ROMANS 15:13 ESV

We're all busy, and we're only getting busier. There is this pervasive societal urge that drives us to fill up our social calendars so that we have no margin to rest, think, or just take a power nap. And if you're feeling lonely, or you're feeling sad about being single, busyness is there to distract you. Couple this with the number of commitments the average woman sustains outside of work and/or school, and it can feel natural to fill any gnawing feelings of emptiness with plans, plans, and more plans.

Of course, there is nothing inherently wrong with being busy, nothing wrong with enjoying a full calendar. Going out to dinner with friends or joining a small group at church are excellent ways for single women to build community and to be reminded that we are not alone in this life. The problem is when we attempt to use our social interactions and busy schedules to fill the void in our hearts. Even being in a relationship won't ensure that you'll never experience loneliness or sadness again. This is because the void we feel in our hearts can be filled only by God. And your relationship with God will deepen by acknowledging your feelings and walking through them while seeking Him for lasting fulfillment.

As Paul writes in Romans, only a relationship with the Lord can fill us with joy, peace, and hope. Only by slowing down and tuning in to the Holy Spirit within us can we listen to our feelings and bring them to God. Busyness itself is not wrong, but if you aren't careful, it can become a slick way to avoid your feelings about your singleness. Busyness can get in the way of the persistent peace He wants to offer you today. Plans are good, but knowing yourself and knowing Him is better.

RIGHT NOW REMINDER:

The hustle will never fill you up
with the sustaining joy that only God can provide.

RELATIONSHIP STATUS IN HEAVEN

*For when the dead rise,
they will neither marry nor be given in marriage.
In this respect they will be like the angels in heaven.*
MARK 12:25 NLT

It may go without saying, but marriage is not a prerequisite to following Christ. For context on today's verse, in Mark 12 the Sadducees are trying to trap Jesus in a debate about the resurrection. The Sadducees were a wealthy religious sect in Jesus' day that used religion to advance their standing in politics. This verse comes at the end of a discussion on religious law and marriage. Isn't it fascinating that Jesus confirms here that when He returns to earth and the dead rise (see Revelation 1:7), marriage will no longer be a factor? Jesus isn't saying that marriage isn't important, as there are many other passages of Scripture that describe the holy imagery and beauty of marriage. Earthly marriage was created as a metaphor to reflect our relationship with God (see Ephesians 5:31–32). He is saying that when He returns to earth to gather up those who believe in Him, "they will neither marry nor be given in marriage." In heaven we will be joined with Christ, and earthly marriage will not be necessary because we will all find our deepest union and satisfaction in Christ.

This is good news for us because it reminds us that God doesn't love those who are in a relationship or are married more than those who are single, and those who are married are not more chosen than the rest of us. And this will be proven true in heaven. Just as the angels in heaven are devoted solely to God, so will we be. Of course, as Scripture tells us, we will be reunited with loved ones in heaven who passed away before us (see I Thessalonians 4:13–18). It will be joyous! And we will be joined together in that joy as we focus our affections on God and live in perfect unity with Him. There will be no dating apps, weddings, or marriages in heaven because our hearts will be at rest in God's love alone. In the meantime, this verse reminds us that Christ values both the married and single relationships one and the same.

RIGHT NOW REMINDER:

Jesus announcing that there is no marriage in heaven reminds us that our identity does not lie in our singleness but ultimately is grounded in our unity and relationship with Him.

SABBATH

Work may be done for six days, but on the seventh day there is to be a Sabbath of complete rest, a sacred assembly. You are not to do any work; it is a Sabbath to the LORD wherever you live.

LEVITICUS 23:3 CSB

We don't live in a culture that values rest. However, in Bible times Sabbath was a part of the culture and was taken very seriously. People were not to work, do housework, study, or even walk farther than absolutely necessary. But what God created as a beautiful rhythm of rest in Genesis 2:2–3 often became a point of contention between Jesus and the Pharisees. They allowed no exceptions to breaking the Sabbath, yet Jesus, in His grace, performed miracles on that day. He knew the Sabbath was important, but His role as the Messiah was even greater (see Matthew 12:9–14). Today, we take the complete opposite approach of the Pharisees by valuing output, to-do lists, and productivity over taking time to rest and reflect.

As a single woman, now is the time to establish your Sabbath routine. Not only will it be life-giving to you in this season, but as your schedule can easily get busier with time, if you have this routine in place, you'll protect the time for rest that you need and flourish all the more.

If the word Sabbath feels a little too intense to you, try "soul care" or "rest and reset." The whole purpose of Sabbath is to slow down enough to hear and process your thoughts (checking in with yourself) and to give yourself space to give those thoughts over to God (reconnecting with Him). Sabbath is personal, so allow yourself to set your own rhythm and pace. Ask God to show you what will bring you soul rest and what will draw you closer to Him. It might look like spending a day off from chores, taking your eyes off your never-ending to-do list, and focusing instead on activities that bring you joy. Maybe it looks like a long walk spent in prayer on your favorite trail followed by a nap and dinner with friends. Maybe it's a morning with a journal and your Bible and an afternoon FaceTiming loved ones who live far away.

Whatever your Sabbath looks like, your singleness affords you time and space to discover what it really means to you. So take advantage and rest well.

RIGHT NOW REMINDER:

Even God rested. Now is your time to establish a Sabbath routine, to slow down and reconnect with yourself and with God.

COMPARING PATHS

Let your eyes look forward;
fix your gaze straight ahead.
Carefully consider the path for your feet,
and all your ways will be established.
Don't turn to the right or to the left;
keep your feet away from evil.
PROVERBS 4:25–27 CSB

We're always comparing. Others have more spending money than we do, but we have a cozier home. This friend has a fast-paced, highly successful career, and we enjoy our job just fine but we work mostly for the weekend. That friend seems unattainably confident in their skin, and we spent last night researching different diets. Comparison seems to be ingrained in us as we assess our lives next to someone else's. Even though our lives are filled with beautiful things, big and small, the lack of a relationship can cause us to feel as though we've come up short. Today's passage exhorts us to cease the comparison game and instead focus on our own path that God is leading us down.

Part of comparison is evaluating if there is enough to go around—enough success, enough happiness, enough love. But just because others around you are in flourishing romantic relationships and solid marriages does not mean the opportunity is gone for you. Theodore Roosevelt once said, "Comparison is the thief of joy." That rings true when you assume that others' relationship success means their life is better than yours—it isn't. If you actively work to focus your eyes on the path God has laid out for you and embrace it as His gift to you, you will find joy untethered from comparison. That is freedom!

RIGHT NOW REMINDER:

Our God is not a God of lack but abundance.
Comparison tempts us to feel that we are lacking,
but God reminds us that He has a path
full of richness and joy laid out just for us.

THE GOD WHO SEES

She gave this name to the LORD who spoke to her:
"You are the God who sees me," for she said,
"I have now seen the One who sees me."
Genesis 16:13 NIV

In today's verse, we are transported into the Old Testament story of a woman named Hagar. Hagar has fled Abraham and Sarai's home after being mistreated, now pregnant with Abraham's son Ishmael. Because of Hagar's abuse at the hands of Abraham and Sarai, she knew they didn't see her as a whole person but only as a surrogate for Abraham's child. She must have felt overlooked and alone, running away to an unknown future because she believed it had to look better than her present circumstances. This is where the angel of the Lord met her—when she was alone, lost, and likely terrified. He calls her "Hagar, servant of Sarai," recognizing her and calling her by name, showing that she is a person of value. The angel of the Lord speaks to her, reassuring her that God has not forgotten her or abandoned her. Not only that, the angel also blesses Hagar and her offspring for generations. Hagar goes away struck with the realization that God saw her. He cared about her life, her experiences, and her heartache. Our God is a God who sees.

While our lives no doubt look very different than Hagar's, we can learn an important lesson from her story. When we feel as though we are going through life alone, when we equate our singleness with our value, and when we feel misunderstood in our feelings of loss, loneliness, or grief over our relationship status, God sees us. Our identity is not tied to our singleness or to another person but rests solely in God. Just as Hagar discovered that her deep need was met in the comfort of God, so can we.

RIGHT NOW REMINDER:

God sees you, right where you are.
However you feel, you are not alone.

WHEN YOU FEEL LIKE YOU ARE GOING THROUGH LIFE ALONE, WHEN YOU EQUATE YOUR SINGLENESS WITH YOUR VALUE, AND WHEN YOU FEEL MISUNDERSTOOD IN YOUR FEELINGS OF LOSS, LONELINESS, OR GRIEF OVER YOUR RELATIONSHIP STATUS,

GOD SEES YOU.

YOUR IDENTITY IS NOT TIED TO YOUR SINGLENESS OR TO ANOTHER PERSON BUT RESTS SOLELY IN GOD.

DEEP AND LASTING FRIENDSHIP

A friend loves at all times,
and a brother is born for adversity.
PROVERBS 17:17 NASB

True friends are with us through thick and thin. We laugh over bowls of pasta on a Monday night watching our favorite reality TV show. We sift through racks side by side at the thrift store, hunting for the perfect outfit for their big presentation at work. We call them up when a first date goes badly, asking for advice and a pep talk because we're feeling discouraged. We help them with all their wedding details, even as we wish we were planning our own ceremony. Friends go through life together—the ups, the downs, and the mundane in-between. And even if you're single and your best friends are not, allowing them to support you through your singleness will only bring you closer.

Just as your dating or married friends freely talk about their significant other, it's important to be honest with them about your experience as a single woman. In fact, if you are vulnerable about your feelings and desires with them, discussing your singleness could become as normal or routine as asking about their boyfriend's new job or discussing date night with their husband. Deep and lasting friendship is not conditional—not on how you act, not on how you look, and not on your relationship status. And, as our verse today reminds us, when you walk through life with your friends, they become more like brothers and sisters to you. Facing adversity, difficulties, and hard times is inevitable. Facing these moments in your singleness is also fairly inescapable. But you never have to face them alone. Whether you are happily single and not looking to change that anytime soon, inching into the dating world with bated breath, or getting comfortable with going on dates, your friends are there to support you. They do not have to be going through the same experience to provide advice, reassurance, or comfort. Be open and honest with your friends about your singleness, and your friendship with these sisters will only deepen.

RIGHT NOW REMINDER:

Even if they are in a different season than you or feel differently about singleness, be honest with your friends about your life and your experience as a single woman. They don't need to be going through the same thing to provide support and encouragement.

JUST AS YOU ARE

*No, in all these things we are
more than conquerors through him who loved us.
For I am sure that neither death nor life,
nor angels nor rulers, nor things present nor things
to come, nor powers, nor height nor depth,
nor anything else in all creation,
will be able to separate us from
the love of God in Christ Jesus our Lord.*
ROMANS 8:37–39 ESV

C. S. Lewis once said, "Though our feelings come and go, God's love for us does not." The love of God toward us is unconditional, meaning there is nothing we can do to lose it, and there is no way He will ever get to a point where He doesn't love us. In the Bible, this type of love is called *agape* love. *Agape* love is the highest form of love, an everlasting and sacrificial love, the type of love that is referenced in I John 4:8 where God is described as the embodiment of love. This love is not rooted in emotions, experiences, or attraction but is a choice to sacrifice and to honor without expecting anything in return. *Agape* love also reminds us that love is not found only in romantic relationships. You are immensely loved just as you are right now by the God of the universe. In fact, you couldn't be more loved than you are right now if you tried!

God demonstrated this *agape* love for us when He sent Jesus to earth to die on the cross, taking on our sins and our shame so that we would have a way to be in relationship with Him. Jesus sacrificed His life for us, even though we did not show love for Him in return. And, as our passage today says, there is absolutely nothing that can get in the way of God's love for us. No matter how we act, what bad choices we make, or what regrets we are trying to forget, God will always love us. As a single woman, be reminded today that the love God has for us is far richer than the romantic love we may desire here on earth.

RIGHT NOW REMINDER:

God loves you with an agape love.
It is unconditional, unyielding, and endless.
Let yourself soak up this truth today.

TREASURES IN HEAVEN

Do not store up for yourselves treasures on earth,
where moths and vermin destroy,
and where thieves break in and steal.
But store up for yourselves treasures in heaven,
where moths and vermin do not destroy,
and where thieves do not break in and steal.
For where your treasure is,
there your heart will be also.
MATTHEW 6:19–21 NIV

As a single woman you carry the burden to pay for everything on your own, and sometimes the list seems endless: rent, groceries, clothes, furniture, pet care, transportation, school. And if your car breaks down or your hand-me-down dresser finally breaks apart, it's on you to find a solution. It's not always easy, and there's something to be said for the skills you learn by managing your money. You should be proud of yourself for doing it on your own! But because of this responsibility, you'll likely find it can be tempting to hold tightly to any money you earn. Of course, saving money and spending wisely are good things, but if there's the temptation to cling to our money, it closes our hearts to generosity and keeps us looking inward. The Bible offers a different perspective: if we store our treasures in heaven, we are able to banish greed from our hearts. Once you begin to be generous with your money, you'll experience the unmitigated joy that comes from giving to others. A joy that is far greater than the joy any new outfit, food delivery, or kitchen gadget can bring.

Our hearts are cheered when we are able to give some of our treasure away, and the more we do it, the more we'll want to do it. You don't have to give large sums of money or give frivolously in order to experience the joy of storing your treasures in heaven. Start small: research a nonprofit that aligns with your passion for adoption or your heart for making sure no one goes hungry, or sponsor a child through Compassion International.* In order to break the cycle of a "treasures on earth" mindset, you just have to start somewhere.

RIGHT NOW REMINDER:

The more you give, the more you'll find that your treasure, your joy, and your delight are in heavenly minded things.

---

* For more information on child sponsorship, visit www.compassion.com.

HEIRS OF HIS KINGDOM

*The Spirit Himself testifies with our spirit that
we are children of God, and if children, heirs also,
heirs of God and fellow heirs with Christ,
if indeed we suffer with Him so that
we may also be glorified with Him.*

ROMANS 8:16–17 NASB

You've likely heard God referred to as God the Father and Jesus as the Son of God. Since God is our Father, we are His children and are designated in Romans as "fellow heirs with Christ." Because of this, we will inherit God's kingdom. What is His kingdom? It's not comprised of a spacious castle, sprawling land, or secret vault filled to the brim with jewels. No, it's better than all of those things put together. The entire universe is God's kingdom: the earth and everything in it, the stars shining brilliantly in the sky, even the galaxies millions of light-years away. And because you have given your life to Him, you have now joined a great community of people who will inherit the universe. And as co-heirs with Christ the Son, what belongs to Jesus belongs to us (see Hebrews 1:2).

Our status as heirs of God's grand creation has only one condition: that we place our trust in Jesus.

We don't need to come from a wealthy family, we don't need to be married with children, we don't need to create a legacy here on earth. Our singleness will never disqualify us from this promise. And because we are God's heirs, we can live life here on earth with the joyful peace that comes with status. An heir to a throne lives with assurance, knowing their status is secure and that riches and favor are theirs. In the same way, we will inherit the vast and magnificent universe alongside Christ. As Colossians 1:12 says, we give "joyful thanks to the Father, who has qualified you to share in the inheritance of his holy people in the kingdom of light" (NIV).

RIGHT NOW REMINDER:

Your singleness will never exclude you from the promise of the inheritance of God's vast and glorious kingdom.

YOU'RE DOING GREAT

Now the Lord is the Spirit,
and where the Spirit of the Lord is,
there is freedom.

II CORINTHIANS 3:17 CSB

In our late teens and early twenties, we have a lot to figure out. How do you open a 401K, and how much should you contribute to it? How do you even do your taxes? How worried should you really be about that weird noise your fridge makes every few days? According to Pew Research, roughly 68 percent of women ages eighteen to twenty-nine are in a relationship. This statistic isn't meant to bum you out but to make you aware: most women have a built-in person to help them get to the bottom of life's issues, run errands with, and work through questions of every kind together. While the fact that you don't have a partner might be hard, it can also be a source of pride. You are doing it all on your own, and you are doing great! You're figuring out how to fix that leak in the pipe under your sink, where to go for the best oil change in town, and what wattage of lightbulb you should buy for the light over your oven. You should be so proud of yourself.

It may feel as though you are solving mundane, necessary problems, but the fact is, a lot of people don't know how to solve these problems because they ask their partner to do it instead. The reality that you do it—and do it well—shows your bravery. Your bravery is on display in everyday life when you are single because you have to figure out all sorts of issues on your own. The fact that you are doing everything yourself right now is amazing. As our verse today says, the Spirit of the Lord is with you through every flat tire, every grocery run, every doctor's appointment—and there is a beautiful independence in this life you are living right now. While you may long for a relationship or marriage one day, you are building character and displaying bravery in your life right now.

RIGHT NOW REMINDER:

You've worked your way through all sorts of issues,
big and small, as a single woman.
You have reason to be proud
of all that you've done.

PERSPECTIVE SHIFT

You must not forget this one thing, dear friends:
A day is like a thousand years to the Lord,
and a thousand years is like a day.
The Lord isn't really being slow about his promise,
as some people think.

II PETER 3:8-9 NLT

When you're single, it's tempting to believe the lie that you're missing out. Maybe you think you're missing out on romance: picture-perfect dates, candlelit dinners, or bonfires under the stars. Or you believe you're being robbed of the life you'd planned out for yourself—a relationship or marriage to lean on as you grew older. Or perhaps you just feel as if you've missed out on the "normal" milestones, having to forge your own path instead. The trouble is, once you begin to buy in to the harmful rhetoric that you're missing out, it can be even more challenging to hear and accept the truth.

It's all about perspective. If your perspective is that you're missing out, you'll feel sadness and the weight of disappointment as you move throughout each day. But if your perspective is that God's got you and the revealing of His plan for your life will be an exciting adventure, you'll be able to open your mind and flourish where you are. This isn't to say that it's wrong to hope and pray for things you desire, like a relationship or marriage. But if you allow yourself to dwell on your lack, you won't see all the good that's in your life. As today's passage explains, our timing is not God's timing. He will reveal His purpose and plans for our lives. In the meantime, we shift our perspective to all the great things: the way a friend's baby giggles over the smallest things, the cozy and safe apartment we return to each night, the pet who is always so excited to see us. We aren't missing out because we are single, and that truth will shift our perspective in an instant.

RIGHT NOW REMINDER:

God has a great plan for your life, and
He is not in a rush to accomplish every bit of it.
The truth is, you are not missing out
just because you are single.

THE PEACE OF GOD

*You will keep the mind that is
dependent on you in perfect peace,
for it is trusting in you.*
ISAIAH 26:3 CSB

We all chase peace. We think that once we achieve that new life goal or make it through this big event, the next season, or an ongoing hardship, peace will suddenly overflow. As single women, many of us probably think that once we find a partner and a romantic relationship, our lives will be easier and our hearts will be more at rest. We buy in to ideas such as "once I have a boyfriend, I'll be happy," "when I'm married, I'll be more content," or "if I'm dating, I'll be less stressed out." But you won't suddenly feel a sense of peace when you're in a relationship. A relationship will not solve your problems, bring you contentment, or suddenly allow you to live a peaceful life. The calm you are looking for can only be found in the Lord.

What does it mean to keep our minds dependent on God? As II Corinthians 10:5 says, we are instructed to take every thought captive to

Christ. Whether you are content with your singleness, actively looking for a relationship, or just trying to decipher your next step in the dating world, a mind dependent on God brings your thoughts, feelings, hopes, and desires to Him. Whether you are going through a hard time in your singleness or are more content with where you are, your mind and heart will feel at peace after communicating with Him through prayer, because He is a God of peace. A prayer as simple as "God, give me Your peace" realigns your mind with Him as you place your trust in Him once again. By giving your life continuously over to Him, you are trusting Him and His plan, knowing that it is better than what you could foresee. You can always ask God for peace when you need it, knowing that He is there for you.

RIGHT NOW REMINDER:

Contentment and peace
don't come from a romantic relationship
but from a consistent pursuit of the peace of God.

A RELATIONSHIP WILL NOT SOLVE YOUR PROBLEMS, BRING YOU CONTENTMENT, OR SUDDENLY ALLOW YOU TO LIVE A PEACEFUL LIFE. **THE PEACE** YOU ARE LOOKING FOR CAN ONLY BE FOUND **IN THE LORD.**

HEALING IS HERE

I am at rest in God alone;
my salvation comes from Him.
He alone is my rock and
my salvation, my stronghold;
I will never be shaken.
PSALM 62:1–2 CSB

Whether you have a complicated family background, struggle with anxiety, have trouble establishing deep friendships, or have experienced any host of other difficulties life throws at you, you know that being human is hard. We've all experienced trauma of some kind, are working through tough situations, or are trying to decipher what all the feelings inside us mean. It can certainly feel overwhelming or discouraging at times. In the midst of the hardship of humanity, it can also be tempting to try to find some sort of Band-Aid to slap on top of it all, helping us to forget our difficulties. For many of us, this Band-Aid takes the form of romantic relationships. But dating and being in a relationship will not heal your wounds or solve your problems. Because dating involves getting attention, validation, compliments, and general good feelings, for a while it might appear to be a healing balm for your soul, helping you to forget about the hard things in life. In reality, you are hurting yourself even more because you are missing the healing the Lord wants to offer you in favor of a quick fix.

Dating and relationships can be a fun distraction, but only God can provide healing. Today's passage reminds us that He is our rock and our foundation—as we look inward, deciphering and working through our traumas and our pain, we can completely trust in Him. Counseling can also be a great tool to consider. God wants healing for you. He wants you to feel uninhibited freedom and love that are rooted in your relationship with Him. He will walk alongside you through every step, not looking to provide a Band-Aid or a way out but serving as your support and a loving, safe presence to be in.

RIGHT NOW REMINDER:

Dating or a relationship will not heal your wounds or solve your problems. Only God can provide the stability and healing you need.

WHOLE AND HIS

You created my innermost parts;
You wove me in my mother's womb.
I will give thanks to You, because I am
awesomely and wonderfully made;
Wonderful are Your works,
and my soul knows it very well.
PSALM 139:13–14 NASB

As a single woman, one of the lies you may be tempted to believe is that you will be made whole once you are in a relationship. This lie is harmful not only because it can cause you to feel even more lonely and set apart in your singleness, but also because it idolizes marriage over singleness, making marriage the answer to your feelings of brokenness. This can cause you to put all your future hope for a whole and healed self on the success of a romantic relationship. While a companion can push you toward a deeper relationship with God and a better version of yourself, they will never complete you. That's because God created you whole and complete as you are right now. You were created by God, awesomely and wonderfully made, lacking nothing.

You were not created as a fragment, looking for its matching piece in the heart of a man. Psalm 139 goes on to say that you were "skillfully formed" by God (v. 15) and "in Your book were written all the days that were ordained for me" (v. 16). God, your Father, created you unique and distinct from 7.7 billion other people on earth. He crafted you with care and sees you as a whole self, planning each and every day of your life here on earth. He did not create you to find all of your fulfillment in someone else but to bring your whole self to Him. Ultimately, you are whole just as you are right now because your identity is in Christ, not in a boyfriend or husband. God's works are wonderful, and you are one of them! You are wonderful because you are His, and no romantic relationship can make that truer.

RIGHT NOW REMINDER:

*You were created whole by God,
and your identity rests in Him.
You are not a fragment waiting to be made
complete by a man.*

UNITY IN CHRIST

There is neither Jew nor Gentile,
neither slave nor free, nor is there male and female,
for you are all one in Christ Jesus.
GALATIANS 3:28 NIV

To us single women, sometimes it feels pretty obvious that our culture values relationships and marriage over singleness. And as we get older, this fact only becomes more apparent. Whether through the assumption that we are dying to get married, the never-ending questions about our dating life from friends, family, and strangers, or our own nagging thoughts that others will think there's something wrong with us because we aren't dating, our status of "single" is constantly questioned, probed at, or dismissed. Our singleness seems to divide us from others, clearly pointing out that we aren't on their level. But God shows us a different way. His is a kingdom of unity.

In Galatians, Paul explains that each and every one of us is a child of God, and because of the saving work of Christ on the cross, we are all united under Him. Some people cannot be ranked higher while others are lower when we are all united in Christ. No one is greater or less than in the kingdom of God. Of course, we are all created different and unique, but we are unified under the banner of Christ instead of being divided by worldly standards. These standards include our relationship status. If you've ever felt defined by your singleness because of the comments of other Christians, those questions or remarks were not from Him. The kingdom of God is a kingdom of unity over division. Colossians 3:14 says that love binds us together in perfect unity. The love of God, and the love that we share with our Christian community, does not accept or reject you based on your relationship status.

RIGHT NOW REMINDER:

We are united in Christ with other believers, and therefore no one is greater or less than in the kingdom of God. Your singleness has not and will not ever disqualify you from this unity.

EVERYONE MAKES MISTAKES

Each time he said, "My grace is all you need.
My power works best in weakness."
So now I am glad to boast about my weaknesses,
so that the power of Christ can work through me.
That's why I take pleasure in my weaknesses,
and in the insults, hardships, persecutions,
and troubles that I suffer for Christ.
For when I am weak, then I am strong.

II CORINTHIANS 12:9 NLT

None of us will walk through our days as single women perfectly. We all make mistakes. We can get too caught up in our sadness over our singleness, we can get too invested in a relationship that isn't right for us, and we can enjoy our independence so much we'll believe we can do life all on our own. We'll mess up, we'll hurt people's feelings, and we'll forget to go to God in our need. But even as we make mistakes, God will always be there for us, extending His powerful and healing grace.

Grace can be defined as God's favor, love, power, and goodness directed toward us—not because of something we did but because of who He is. Grace is more than salvation; it also encompasses everything we need for life and to pursue godliness. Our weakness actually increases our need for grace, displaying the power of Christ in us. Our weakness is never truly that, because in our mistakes we meet the grace of God. Don't be afraid of your mistakes, as they are an opportunity for you to receive and experience the grace of God. They are also not an indication of failure or a reason for your singleness. Your mistakes are instead an indication that you need God and His saving grace.

RIGHT NOW REMINDER:

You won't walk through this season
of singleness perfectly, and that's okay.
God's grace will meet you in every mistake,
strengthening you for the journey ahead.

FOR GOD'S GLORY

*Avoid immorality. Any other sin
a man commits does not affect his body;
but the man who is guilty of sexual immorality sins
against his own body. Don't you know that your body
is the temple of the Holy Spirit, who lives in you and
who was given to you by God? You do not belong to
yourselves but to God; he bought you for a price.
So use your bodies for God's glory.*
I CORINTHIANS 6:18–20 GNT

God has called us to flee from sexual immortality. In the Christian culture especially, this topic is often avoided because it is deemed too awkward to be discussed. But as single women who are bombarded with messages in movies, TV, and music that preach the opposite of honoring God with our bodies, we have to be in tune with and aware of what the Bible says on this topic. The basis for avoiding sexual immorality is spelled out here in verse 19, which says our bodies are temples (vessels) of the Holy Spirit. Verse 20 goes on to say that we were bought with a price, the price being Christ's death on a cross. Our bodies have been delivered from the punishment of our sins because of Christ. Giving in to temptation of any kind as a single person only leads us to guilt and further temptation, but honoring God with our bodies reminds us that we ultimately belong to Him.

Sexual sin only destroys, and we are called to resist and run away from it (see I Thessalonians 4:3–5). If you've made mistakes in the past, remember that the Lord is a loving and forgiving God (see Psalm 86:5). The more you resist temptation and seek to honor God with your body, the easier it will become. As Sam Allbery writes, "As we strive to be faithful to Him, often in the midst of an unsympathetic and scornful world, He sees us. Our labors for Him are never unnoticed." You can see your body as a vessel for God's glory as you walk through your days as a single woman, leaning on Him when you need strength to avoid immorality.

RIGHT NOW REMINDER:

It's important to God that
we use our bodies for His glory,
not giving in to temporary temptations.

LIFE IS BEAUTIFUL

He has made everything beautiful in its time.
Also, he has put eternity into man's heart,
yet so that he cannot find out what
God has done from the beginning to the end.
ECCLESIASTES 3:11 ESV

When we get right down to it, our core fear as single women is that our singleness is going to last forever. What feelings follow this line of thinking look a little different for different people, but it's probably something like dread, anxiety, sadness, or fear. We feel these hard emotions because we think that the most beautiful things in our lives will be the result of a happy relationship, but that just isn't true. Yes, relationships, dating, and marriage can certainly add value to one's life. But they are just a small part of all the good we can do, beauty we can experience, and life we can live here on earth. Regardless of whether your singleness lasts for another day, month, year, or lifetime, you can live a flourishing and fulfilled life here and now.

Life is so beautiful. From the bitter cold sunrise in Alaska, where the world looks shiny and crisp, to the hazy sunsets on the serene beaches of Mykonos. From the arctic snow leopard kittens making their home in the mountains of India to the zebras on the plains of Mozambique. Even your own neighborhood is teeming with life: flowers and weeds coming up in a messy splendor on the corner, dogs happily trotting alongside their owners on the street, the warm sun streaming through the new spring buds on the trees. Your life is so complex and beautiful, and there is only more goodness to be found. As our passage today explains, God has set eternity in our heart. As we look forward to spending forever with Him, let us have eyes to see the beauty and goodness that surround us today. Don't allow your fear of your singleness lasting longer than you'd like it to hold you back from seeing the richness of life today.

RIGHT NOW REMINDER:

*There is happiness, beauty, and joy
to be found in your life right now.
You don't have to wait until you are
in a relationship to experience these things.*

OUR SOURCE OF LIFE

*Jesus said, "Everyone who drinks from this water
will get thirsty again. But whoever drinks from the water
that I will give him will never get thirsty again.
In fact, the water I will give him will become
a well of water springing up in him for eternal life."*

JOHN 4:13–14 CSB

Good friendships and deep relationships bring life. Whether you are an introvert, an extrovert, or somewhere in between, feeling known by someone else is encouraging to your soul and uplifting to your spirit. And while relationships on earth can and do bring life, this is ultimately a fraction of the life and joy you can find in Jesus, the wellspring of eternal life. He knows you better than anyone else.

In John 4, Jesus encounters a Samaritan woman at a well, and when He speaks to her, He reveals both the reality of His identity as Messiah and the truth that she doesn't need to look elsewhere for life when her Savior is right in front of her. This would have been joyous news for the Samaritan woman because her past had been filled with hurt and broken relationships, as she reveals to Jesus that she has been married five times and is now living with a new man. But none of these relationships have satisfied the longing in her soul. In our passage today, Jesus explains to her that the true source of life is Him alone.

Just like the Samaritan woman, we can go looking for fulfillment in many different places. And as single women, it's easy to believe in our daydreaming, that if we just met the right person, our lives would be changed. But when our source of life is not found in Jesus, we will always be left high and dry. Another person can only provide us with so much. Instead, if we root ourselves in Jesus as our source of life, our relationships of all kinds will reflect the abundance He offers us.

RIGHT NOW REMINDER:

Jesus is our source of life,
not a significant other.

THIS LOVE IS FOR US

So now faith, hope, and love abide, these three; but the greatest of these is love.
I CORINTHIANS 13:13 ESV

First Corinthians 13 is often referred to as "the love chapter." It's quoted at weddings, slapped on picture frames, and embroidered on pillows—and for good reason. This chapter of the Bible describes love in a beautiful way: "Love is patient and kind; love does not envy or boast; it is not arrogant or rude. It does not insist on its own way; it is not irritable or resentful; it does not rejoice at wrongdoing but rejoices with the truth. Love bears all things, believes all things, hopes all things, endures all things" (vv. 4–7 ESV). The thing is, nowhere in this chapter is this kind of self-sacrificing, life-sustaining love ascribed to a romantic relationship. While the wedding industry may have tried to co-opt this chapter for its own purposes, we, too, can claim this kind of love in our lives today.

It starts with understanding that God loves us with this kind of love right now, and there is nothing we can do to lose or lessen that love. We have each also been gifted with friends and family we love and who love us. The deep love we share with our closest friends is called *phileo* love. Jesus demonstrated this *phileo* love when He wept over the death of His friend Lazarus. Upon seeing Jesus' reaction, those around Him remarked, "See how he loved him!" (John 11:36 ESV). With family, either biological or chosen, we experience *storge* love, which is loyal, persistent, and patient. When Mary and Martha grieved over that same loss of their brother Lazarus in John 11:1–44, their grief came from a place of *storge* love. And the highest form of love, *agape* love, is shown in today's passage. God's deep and unending love for us demonstrates for us how we can love others. You do not need to be getting married in order to give and receive the love described in I Corinthians 13. As we receive God's love, we will learn how to love others well.

RIGHT NOW REMINDER:

*Being loved is a promise and
a reality for you right now.
You do not need to wait
until you recite your vows
to give and receive love.*

PROVERBS 31 WOMEN

She is clothed with strength and dignity,
and she laughs without fear of the future.
PROVERBS 31:25 NLT

Proverbs 31:10–31 is titled "In praise of the wife of noble character." Throughout the passage, the attributes of this wife are described: savvy, brave, generous, caring. She is a hardworking businesswoman, a problem solver, and a thinker. And just as we glean truths from David when he steps into bravery and slays Goliath or from Noah when he follows God's orders to build the ark before the storm clouds even roll in, we can learn from the wisdom of the Proverbs 31 woman. We are single women, and we are Proverbs 31 women. We do not have to wait for marriage or a family to be an example to others of strength, dignity, and love.

In Proverbs 31, God is the undercurrent of the woman's success. Throughout her various activities, she follows the Lord closely and is concerned about bringing Him glory. Verse 30 even says, "Charm is deceptive, and beauty does not last; but a woman who fears the LORD will be greatly praised." If you want to be like her, you can start by shifting your perspective to working throughout each day to bring God glory. Whether you are working at your nine-to-five, cleaning your room, or volunteering in the community, you can mimic the Proverbs 31 woman's commitment to God in every single project you undertake. Her strength and her dignity are an outpouring of her relationship with God, and that goodness touches each of her interactions with those around her, as well as her actions in her work and household. Similarly, God has clothed you with strength and dignity as His child. You are dignified, and you are strong. So we develop our noble character today, not so that it will help us get a man but so that we can be the best version of who God has created us to be and reflect His glory to those around us.

RIGHT NOW REMINDER:

You are a Proverbs 31 woman.
When you are secure in Him,
you will reflect His glory to those around you,
just like the wife of noble character.

WE ARE SINGLE WOMEN, AND
WE ARE PROVERBS 31 WOMEN.
WE DO NOT HAVE TO WAIT FOR
MARRIAGE OR A FAMILY TO BE
AN EXAMPLE TO OTHERS OF
STRENGTH, DIGNITY,
AND LOVE.

YOU ARE NOT FAILING

God is within her, she will not fall;
God will help her at break of day.
PSALM 46:5 NIV

Maybe you have a cringey first date story that you bust out at a girls' night when everyone needs a good laugh. Or perhaps your heart is still tender and healing from a previous relationship that you thought might last forever. Or it could be that dating just hasn't been your priority, and you haven't been on more than a few mediocre dates. No matter what is true for you, as a single woman it can feel tempting to compare your dating history to those around you and feel as if you don't measure up. Rest assured, whether you've had more heartbreaks and exes than you care to recount, or you haven't had a boyfriend before, God's grace is there to help us navigate the world of singleness, dating, and relationships. Being single does not mean you have failed in some way. God does not look at you and see failure. He sees His beloved daughter whom He empowers with His strength and assurance. Today's verse reminds us of that truth.

And because God is with you as well as dwelling within you through the Holy Spirit, you will not fall, you will not fail. The ESV translates this part of Psalm 46:5 to "she shall not be moved," and the CSB describes it as "she will not be toppled." The strength of the Lord is within you. The Creator of the universe attends to your heart and will provide you with the reassurance, hope, and perseverance you need. Earlier in Psalm 46, God is described as "our refuge and strength, an ever-present help in trouble" (v. 1). God will help you through your season of singleness. Whether you feel disappointed, anticipatory, or content in this time, your singleness does not reflect failure as a person in any way.

RIGHT NOW REMINDER:

Your singleness does not indicate some kind of failure. God's strength can and will empower you as you navigate this season.

THE JEALOUSY TRAP

If in your heart you are jealous, bitter, and selfish,
don't sin against the truth by boasting of your wisdom.
JAMES 3:14 GNT

We all know someone who seems like they have it all together. Maybe they're always on time, showing up to dinner with effortlessly simple hair and makeup and a perfectly put-together outfit. Or they have an amazing career, traveling across the country and climbing the corporate ladder with apparent ease. Or they seem to have the best relationship, a boyfriend or spouse that they gush about and always post on-point selfies with. No matter what it is, their life seems somewhat uncomplicated, graceful, and enviable. When we put someone on a pedestal of perfection—a friend, a family member, or even a stranger—it's inevitable that we will compare their life to our own and come up wanting. We see something in them that we desire, and jealousy sets in.

The thing about jealousy is that it only hurts us. When we are jealous, we are downgrading our own blessings and our own successes, and we are hurting our relationship with the person we envy. This is especially true when it comes to jealousy over someone else's romantic relationship. Whether we are jealous over a friend's new boyfriend, a high school acquaintance's beautiful engagement, or a cousin's boho wedding, jealousy turns our hearts bitter and blocks us from the wisdom of God. God detests jealousy because it is the opposite of thankfulness, the opposite of praising Him for His plan for our lives. When we feel the spark of jealousy in our hearts, let us turn immediately to gratefulness for our own path. And then we can simultaneously be happy for someone's success without allowing it to reflect on our own lives. We can be happy for them and happy for us.

RIGHT NOW REMINDER:

Jealousy only hurts us,
but gratitude and thankfulness are the cure.
Be on guard against envy
in your own heart today and try to refocus
on the God-given good in your own life.

JAEL'S STORY

When Barak arrived in pursuit of Sisera,
Jael went out to greet him and said to him,
"Come and I will show you the man you are
looking for." So he went in with her, and there was
Sisera lying dead with a tent peg through his temple!
JUDGES 4:22 CSB

What does a woman who follows God look like? You may look around and see that many of your friends are different than you, maybe gentler, kinder, or more soft-spoken. You may compare your actions to those who are more generous or thoughtful. And as a single woman, you may equate these traits not only with godliness but with success in romantic relationships. But our Bible passage today reminds us that there is not one type of godly woman. Godly women can be patient, nurturing, and soft, and they can also be bold, powerful, and brave.

Let's set the stage: In Judges 4, Israel was at war with the Canaanites. Deborah was the judge over Israel, and she appointed a man named Barak to lead Israel's army. Sisera was his adversary, the commander of the Canaanite army. When Deborah tells Barak to prepare for battle against Sisera, he responds, "If you will go with me, I will go. But if you will not go with me, I will not go" (v. 8). Deborah agrees to this but explains that Barak will not get the glory of defeating Sisera because he responded in this way. In battle, Sisera's army is losing, and he flees and ends up hiding in Jael's tent. She is a smart and daring woman, making Sisera comfortable by giving him a blanket and milk to drink. But after he falls asleep, she seizes the opportunity and drives a tent peg into his temple, securing victory for the Israelites. This was the beginning of the end of the Canaanites' rule over Israel.

Jael doesn't fit the model of what many of us think a biblical woman looks like. And yet, here she is: a courageous woman in Scripture. God made you unique for a reason, and your particular traits will influence your success in romantic relationships but not necessarily dictate them. May Jael's story remind you today that God doesn't call you to fit into a certain mold.

RIGHT NOW REMINDER:
God created you for you.
You are powerful, brave, and courageous!

FAMILY

Father to the fatherless, defender of widows—
this is God, whose dwelling is holy.
God places the lonely in families;
he sets the prisoners free and gives them joy.

PSALM 68:5–6 NLT

You are a part of a big family, filled with children to raise, elders to learn from, and brothers and sisters to grow with. As a single woman, this can be a difficult truth to wrap your mind around. Especially as you get older and your married friends start to have kids, it can feel as if you are being left behind. Many of them draw in closer, forming a tight-knit circle that feels impenetrable. But the truth is, your friends want your help, your love, your presence in their family. Oftentimes friends with spouses and/or kids feel like you might not be interested in being a part of their fast-paced, slightly chaotic days. And at the same time, you feel as though they are a unit not in need of another hand. But God has a vision of family for you here today. The definition of family isn't tied to marriage or children but to wholeness and to unity in Christ.

Jesus Himself paints a broader picture of family

in Mark when He says: "'Who is my mother? Who are my brothers?' Then he looked at those around him and said, 'Look, these are my mother and brothers. Anyone who does God's will is my brother and sister and mother'" (Mark 3:33–35 NLT). As followers of Christ, we are a part of a beautiful, giant, and fun and crazy family. And the best way to take hold of this promise is to be honest with your friends, let them know that you long for family, and ask to be a part of their family routines. Bring dinner over once a week and eat together, young kids throwing food and interrupting left and right. Go to one of their children's soccer games, getting to know the other parents on the sidelines and bringing snacks for everyone. Help organize the kitchen or the kids' rooms after church one day alongside your friends. As we broaden our definition of family, we will see God's plan for our inherited families come to fruition.

RIGHT NOW REMINDER:

Scripture shows us that the idea of family isn't synonymous with marriage or children but finds its fullness in Christ. You are a part of a family.

PURE OF HEART

How can a young man keep his way pure?
By guarding it according to your word.
With my whole heart I seek you;
let me not wander from your commandments!

PSALM 119:9–10 ESV

Many of us grew up with a warped definition of purity. Oftentimes our culture defines purity as the way we dress, the way we act, and who we do or don't hang around with. Sometimes the emphasis is put on how we affect someone else's purity too, particularly how we as women affect men. The pressure can be placed on women to dress or act a certain way so that we don't tempt men to sin in thought or action. But as today's passage reminds us, purity is based in God's Word and is each person's own responsibility. And this is how the Bible describes purity: a personal conviction and pursuit that is the opposite of sexual immorality.

"For this is the will of God, your sanctification: that you abstain from sexual immorality; that each one of you know how to control his own body in holiness and honor" (I Thessalonians 4:3–4 ESV). Notice here that the Bible speaks on purity only as an individual conviction and pursuit, not as something you are in charge of for someone else. We are not responsible for anyone else's thoughts or actions and whether they are pure or not. We are called to keep our own hearts pure, yes, but this is something only God can determine. Your purity is also not, nor will it ever be, based on how others view you. It is instead grounded in your relationship with the Lord and living your life as the Bible instructs. The opposite of purity are the works of the flesh, meaning living according to our human desires as opposed to God's Word (see Galatians 5:19–21).

Purity doesn't lie in how you dress, how you do your makeup, how you act, or in how any of this affects someone else's life. It lies in your heart. And you are not responsible to uphold someone else's view on purity—each person must be responsible for themselves. As single women, we can pursue a life of purity while freeing ourselves from the pressure that we must guard others' heart and minds to keep them on the path of purity as well.

RIGHT NOW REMINDER:

Purity is based in God's Word.
As a single woman, you are not responsible
for anyone's purity but your own.

SEASONS OF SINGLENESS

*There is a time for everything, and
a season for every activity under the heavens.*
ECCLESIASTES 3:1 NIV

Do you feel as though your singleness will last forever or wonder if you'll ever find someone special? The fact is, as of 2021, 91 percent of Americans sixty and older have been married. So statistically speaking, you will probably get married at *some* point in your lifetime. In your most lonely and sad moments of singleness, this statistic can be of great encouragement. And even in your moments of contentment or peace, this statistic tells us that singleness is just one of the many stages of your life. As you probably know by now, life has many seasons, trials, joys, celebrations, and hardships. Among the different times of life listed in Ecclesiastes are "a time to be born and a time to die, a time to plant and a time to uproot . . . a time to tear down and a time to build, a time to weep and a time to laugh, a time to mourn and a time to dance . . . a time to embrace and a time to refrain from embracing, a time to search and a time to give up, a time to keep and a time to throw away" (vv. 2–6 NIV). With this perspective, why not delve into contentment, joy, and the opportunities that abound here and now in your season of singleness?

Whether you get married in the future or not, your season of life is bound to change. If you are struggling with your singleness, may this offer a balm to your soul. God has not left you alone, and He knows the desires of your heart (see Psalm 37:4). If you are happily single, you're in a season to invest—in yourself, in your community, and in your relationship with God. If you're investigating your feelings about your singleness, now may be either "a time to embrace or a time to refrain from embracing." Ask God to lead you in this season, and He will direct your path. However you feel about your life as a single woman, remember that this is just one of the seasons of life.

RIGHT NOW REMINDER:

Singleness is one of many different seasons that makes up your full and beautiful life.

GOD OUR HELPER

I lift up my eyes to the mountains—
where does my help come from?
My help comes from the LORD,
the Maker of heaven and earth.
PSALM 121:1–2 NIV

Single women are powerful. No matter what life stage you're in, whether you're a student, beginning your career, or settled and successful, you've had to navigate adulthood on your own. From broken pipes to electric bills, from budgeting to meal planning, you've taken on the full gamut of what life brings. And you should be so proud of yourself. You are an independent woman, and you are crushing it. Being independent is a beautiful thing, and growing this skill is one of the benefits of singleness.

Trouble comes in, however, when we examine our own hearts and find that we have become so independent that we don't think we need help even from God. When this happens, your internal dialogue shifts from "God is with me, I can be brave" to "I can do it on my own." But the fact is, we can't do life all on our own. Today's passage reminds us that we can be independent women who are dependent on God.

Independent woman who are dependent on God seems like an oxymoron, right? But the fact is that you can cherish your freedom, dwell in bravery, and push yourself outside of your comfort zone into new experiences . . . and still rely on God. Dependence on God is the gasoline that fuels your adventurous life as a single woman. The Creator of the heavens and the earth wants to stand by your side, offering you help whenever you call upon Him. And it's always okay to ask God for help. Even though you're single, an independent queen, you don't have to do anything all on your own. Psalm 54:4 says, "Surely God is my help; the Lord is the one who sustains me" (NIV). You will need help throughout your season of singleness, and that doesn't diminish your independent spirit in the slightest.

RIGHT NOW REMINDER:

Dependence on God will power your independence. He is your helper.

UNANSWERED PRAYERS

This is the confidence we have before Him:
If we ask anything according to His will,
He hears us.
I JOHN 5:14 CSB

How do we deal with the reality of unanswered prayers? Maybe you've been praying diligently for a relationship and an end to your singleness for months or years. Maybe you don't even pray about your singleness anymore, feeling fed up and confused. How do you work through the truth that God wants what's best for you when you feel this ache in your own heart, a strong and at times all-consuming desire for companionship? Many people in the Bible also questioned if their prayers were being heard by a loving, kind God. Job suffered greatly, having lost everything he had. In Job 30:20 he says of God, "I cry out to you for help, but you do not answer me; when I stand up, you merely look at me" (CSB). Paul repeatedly asked God to remove his "thorn in the flesh" (see II Corinthians 12:6–9). Yet he suffered from this struggle for his entire life. The church prayed for the apostle Peter's release from prison day after day, until he was finally delivered from prison by an angel of the

Lord (Acts 12:1–19). You are not alone if you feel exasperated by your unanswered prayers. While they remain unanswered, take comfort in knowing that God hears you and is working everything out for your good (see Romans 8:28).

First Peter 5:10 says, "The God of all grace, who called you to his eternal glory in Christ, will himself restore, establish, strengthen, and support you after you have suffered a little while" (CSB). Your unanswered prayers may feel like suffering, abandonment, or hopelessness. But you have not been left alone; you are not speaking to the ceiling or praying into the void. Our passage today in I John 5:14 tells us that God hears us. He listens and He cares. God has promised to restore, support, and strengthen you in and through your singleness. God does not turn a deaf ear; He receives the burdens of our hearts with open arms.

RIGHT NOW REMINDER:

*Even if you feel like your prayers
are going unheard, they aren't.
God hears you and cares for you.*

SHIPHRAH AND PUAH

Then Pharaoh, the king of Egypt, gave this order to the Hebrew midwives, Shiphrah and Puah: "When you help the Hebrew women as they give birth, watch as they deliver. If the baby is a boy, kill him; if it is a girl, let her live." But because the midwives feared God, they refused to obey the king's orders. They allowed the boys to live, too. So the king of Egypt called for the midwives. "Why have you done this?" he demanded. "Why have you allowed the boys to live?" "The Hebrew women are not like the Egyptian women," the midwives replied. "They are more vigorous and have their babies so quickly that we cannot get there in time." So God was good to the midwives, and the Israelites continued to multiply, growing more and more powerful. And because the midwives feared God, He gave them families of their own.

EXODUS 1:15–21 NLT

There are plenty of single women in Scripture who inspire us to bravery, to living a God-given adventure in the here and now. Today's story is set in a time when Israel, God's people, was enslaved and abused by the Egyptians. In the midst of this mistreatment, two presumably single women,

Shiphrah and Puah, demonstrate extraordinary bravery. As midwives, they see their opportunity to further God's plan instead of going along with the king's decree. So they go against Pharoah's orders, risking their own lives to spare the lives of an untold number of Israelite boys. They didn't consider themselves less than because of their singleness, and they didn't wait to consult another person. They knew what God was calling them to do and acted with remarkable courage.

All of Israel was blessed by Shiphrah and Puah, and they were in turn blessed with families of their own. They walked closely with the Lord, and He was good to them. It all began because they listened to the will of God. God used these seemingly inconsequential single women to change history and to be a part of delivering His people from bondage.

RIGHT NOW REMINDER:

God can use you
in miraculous ways as a single woman.

RESISTING LIES

Finally, build up your strength in union with the Lord and by means of His mighty power. Put on all the armor that God gives you, so that you will be able to stand up against the Devil's evil tricks. For we are not fighting against human beings but against the wicked spiritual forces in the heavenly world, the rulers, authorities, and cosmic powers of this dark age. So put on God's armor now! Then when the evil day comes, you will be able to resist the enemy's attacks; and after fighting to the end, you will still hold your ground.

EPHESIANS 6:10–13 GNT

It's hard to resist the soundtrack of lies that can play in your mind surrounding singleness. When lies like "you are unlovable," "you're single because of X, Y, or Z," or "you'll never find someone who loves you for you" echo day after day, it's no wonder you feel discouraged about your singleness. But these messages are not from your loving Father, who has a beautiful plan for your life. Instead, they are lies from Satan, who is called the father of lies in John 8. Satan uses upsetting tactics such as these to wear you down and try to get you to lose faith in God and in His plan. Satan will lie to you about yourself and about your singleness, but you are not left alone to fight these falsehoods. God has equipped you with His Spirit and His power to stand up to these disheartening attacks.

Recognizing lies about your relationship status is the first step to fighting them. When you can see these untruths for what they are, you realize that the enemy is working against you. In these moments, you can reject him with a phrase as simple as "God is with me, the devil has no power here" or "God is more powerful than Satan will ever be. I reject the enemy's lies." God wants to provide you with courage to stand up to the devil's tricks, resisting them and finding the peace and joy that are in Christ instead. Whenever you feel particularly discouraged about your singleness, assess whether you've been allowing some harmful lies to seep in.

RIGHT NOW REMINDER:

The devil will try to discourage you,
but the Lord is infinitely more powerful
to encourage you in your season of singleness.

KNOWING YOURSELF

Are not two sparrows sold for a penny?
Yet not one of them will fall to the ground outside
your Father's care. And even the very hairs of
your head are all numbered. So don't be afraid;
you are worth more than many sparrows.
MATTHEW 10:29–31 NIV

One of the greatest things about singleness is the time and space it provides to really get to know yourself. Whether you have roommates, live with family, or live alone, no matter your schedule, you will spend more time alone in this season than most others in life. That time is a gift—time to think, to process, and to mine the depths of your own heart and mind. Sure, it is a big undertaking to learn more about who you are, how your past and present formed you, and parts of yourself that you love or that you'd like to work through. But learning more about the complexities that make up you is the most rewarding adventure you can take, and now is your time. Talking to a professional through therapy can be really helpful and healing here, and of course finding friends and family members to confide in is extremely valuable as well. Don't let your fear of what you'll uncover stop you from finding out who you really are.

God is with you every step of the way. He delights in the moments that you grow deeper into who He created you to be, and He longs for you to know your true self as He does. As a single woman, now is your time to flourish. This opportunity is a gift, and if you will take advantage of it, you'll find healing, hope, and contentment. You'll find yourself. You'll find the reassurance that you have infinite worth, you are lovable, and you will be okay. As today's passage reminds us, you can never fall outside the realm of God's love. You are worthy of self-discovery and growth. You are worthy of love as you are today, single and not sorry.

RIGHT NOW REMINDER:

If you embark on the journey of self-discovery, you'll find healing, hope, and contentment— all rooted in God's love for you. You are worthy of good things.

YOU CAN NEVER FALL OUTSIDE THE REALM OF GOD'S LOVE. YOU ARE WORTHY OF SELF-DISCOVERY AND GROWTH. YOU ARE WORTHY OF LOVE AS YOU ARE TODAY, SINGLE AND NOT SORRY.

RAHAB

"Now swear to me by the Lord that you will be kind to me and my family since I have helped you. Give me some guarantee that when Jericho is conquered, you will let me live, along with my father and mother, my brothers and sisters, and all their families." "We offer our own lives as a guarantee for your safety," the men agreed. "If you don't betray us, we will keep our promise and be kind to you when the Lord gives us the land."
JOSHUA 2:12–14 NLT

Single women are brave, are empowered by God, and are situated to do extraordinary things. Today's passage puts us in the middle of the story of a single woman named Rahab who embodied these things. Rahab was a Canaanite prostitute, an enemy of the Israelites. However, when two Israelite spies went to scope out the city of Jericho, where Rahab lived, she protected them from being caught and facing certain death. She risked her own life to protect the Israelite spies, knowing that they must have been sent there by God. This would have been shocking to the original audience of the book of Joshua! Rahab had no reason or motivation to save these men other than God-ordained intervention and God-given insight.

And because she rescued them, when they returned to conquer Jericho, her life was spared, along with her family's.

Because her agreement with the spies makes no mention of sparing her husband, it's safe to assume she was single at the time. Rahab recognized that God was powerful and unstoppable, and she went against her own people because she sensed that He was ultimately in control. That took incredible courage. We can model our own lives after the bravery of Rahab, rooting our decisions in the power of God. Later, in Hebrews 11, Rahab is recognized as a hero of the faith: "It was by faith that Rahab the prostitute was not destroyed with the people in her city who refused to obey God. For she had given a friendly welcome to the spies" (Hebrews 11:31 NLT). Rahab aligned herself with the Lord and will forever be remembered for her heroism and faith.

RIGHT NOW REMINDER:

You won't be remembered for your singleness. You'll be remembered for your faith in God and your brave acts of courage, empowered by Him.

STIRRING UP LOVE

Do not stir up or awaken love
until the appropriate time.
SONG OF SONGS 2:7 CSB

The world likes to remind you that you're missing out on romantic love. There's always a new rom-com coming out, a trending love song on repeat, a new reality dating show everyone's talking about. There are couples strolling past you on the sidewalk holding hands, friends starting relationships or getting married, and social media's post after post preaching how wonderful it is to be in love. Someday the type of romantic love these songs are written about, these shows are based on, and these movies are created for might be a reflection of your life but only if and when the time is right.

Song of Songs actually reminds us three times throughout the book that we should not awaken love until the time is right (2:7, 3:5, 8:4). For a book of the Bible all about love, it's interesting that this word of caution is included. It's included because it serves as a sobering reminder to us single women: romantic love can be a beautiful, healing, and amazing thing, but if we chase after it before the time is right, it will only hurt us. Awakening love too soon could look like pursuing romantic relationships even if it feels like the wrong time or something just feels off, going too far physically in a dating relationship because you're caught up in your feelings, or allowing your mind to obsess about love (or the lack of it) because you feel as if you're missing out. It's hard to trust that God has a plan for you—even when it feels like the world is falling in love around you—but He will bring romantic love into your life at the right time. So while you wait, it's your time to cultivate your community and deepen your relationship with Him. You're not missing out on romantic love, you're following God's timing and fully embracing the most amazing love you'll ever know—His!

RIGHT NOW REMINDER:

If you pursue romantic love outside of God's plan,
you will compromise the very best He has for you.
If romantic love is in His plan for you,
He will orchestrate it in His perfect time.

THE DISCIPLES

Don't we have the right to be accompanied
by a believing wife like the other apostles,
the Lord's brothers, and Cephas?
I CORINTHIANS 9:5 CSB

The inner circle of Jesus was comprised of His disciples: James (the younger), Philip, Judas, Jude (or Thaddeus), John, James, Andrew, Peter (or Cephas), Simon, Thomas, Matthew (or Levi) and Bartholomew. These twelve men traveled miles upon miles with Jesus in their dusty worn sandals, talked and laughed over meals with Jesus, and slept next to Him in front of the fire on cold and cloudless nights. They saw Jesus do miracles, heal the sick, and bring joy to the downtrodden. They also saw Him tired after a long journey, frustrated, and discouraged. They were Jesus' trusted confidants, His deepest community here on earth. They were Jesus' best friends, and He loved them greatly (see John 15:12). And, as far as we know, only one of them was married.

The fact that only one of Jesus' disciples, Peter (also known as Cephas), was married affirms for us that Jesus does not see marriage as a qualification for a full, God-honoring life. While the church today may emphasize the importance of marriage, sometimes insinuating it is essential, most of Jesus' closest friends here on earth were single. Our culture today tells us that you are a holier, more fulfilled Christian when you are married. Our skewed view zeros in on the Scripture passages on marriage, while ignoring the numerous examples of powerful world-changers in the Word who never walked down the aisle. Jesus' disciples walked the earth with Him, saw Him crucified, and saw Him rise again. They spent hours, days, years with our Savior. And Jesus never once spoke to them on the necessity of marriage. As today's verse explains, marriage is a gift but never a requirement. The disciples were free to marry, but they were not pressured to. Therefore, Jesus did not and does not see it as a prerequisite for a life that glorifies Him.

RIGHT NOW REMINDER:

Jesus' closest community here on earth was filled with people who were unmarried. A Spirit-filled, God-honoring life does not have to include a husband.

GOD'S PLAN

*Whatever is good and perfect is
a gift coming down to us from God our Father,
who created all the lights in the heavens.
He never changes or casts a shifting shadow.*
JAMES 1:17 NLT

God is not manipulated by us, by our human will. We can get stuck in an unhealthy mindset as single women that goes something like this: "If I date enough men, God will see that I'm trying, and I'm sure to find the right one!" or "If I tell enough people about my desire to be married, God will know that I'm serious about it!" or even "My struggle with singleness is pretty clear. I've suffered long enough, and God should get that!" These subtle messages may even be buried in your subconscious, but they're there, putting you at odds with the goodness of God's plan. We've all felt this, whether we like to admit it or not. But instead of feeling that tug of desperation that pulls you into a mindset that tells God what He "should" be doing, we can remind ourselves that the good gift of a relationship will come from Him and in His timing.

You aren't going to find the best person for you apart from the will of God. He isn't going to change His mind because you want Him to. And instead of getting discouraged as a single woman, what if this propelled you to flourish in your singleness now? Because you cannot manipulate God, you can only dwell in the here and now. Instead of trying to convince God that you are worthy of a romantic relationship, lean into His promise to hear the desires of your heart (see Psalm 37:4). He knows everything about you, He knows your preferred timetable, He knows all your feelings. He wants to reveal the gifts in your life here and now, while you wait for the gift of a partner. He will not change, even as you do. You can lean on Him, looking to discover His goodness in your everyday, knowing that He sees you.

RIGHT NOW REMINDER:

You can't manipulate God, and
you aren't going to fall into a relationship
that's got His hand of favor on it outside of His will.
Rest in His plan today, knowing that
He sees you and your desires.

LIKE WHAT YOU LIKE

For we are his workmanship,
created in Christ Jesus for good works,
which God prepared beforehand,
that we should walk in them.
EPHESIANS 2:10 ESV

Don't change yourself for someone else. Sounds pretty obvious, right? But sometimes, when we really want to be in a romantic relationship, we distort the truth because we want to relate to the other person, we want them to like us back, and we ultimately want their approval. So we lie about how often we listen to that indie folk band or if we've played this video game or not, or we don't reveal how much we really love cats. We put pressure on ourselves to morph into what we think others will like, forgetting the things in our lives that bring us joy because we think a relationship will outweigh any joy we currently feel. But we have so many good things in our lives now to embrace, practice, and try that will fill us with joy!

So like what you like. God has given you a splendor of preferences, tastes, and loves, big and small, that bring your life color, show your uniqueness, and can be a source of infinite joy. Embrace them, and don't try to change what you like for someone else. You were created by God for good works, works that flow out of your passion for music, your love for nature, or your desire to create. Do you love animals? Adopt a kitten, volunteer at your local animal shelter, buy a cat T-shirt. Is your happy place found in the pages of a new book? Join a book club, get your library card, volunteer at the local library's events. Do you want to bake more? Watch tutorials, try out different recipes, give your bakes to friends to be your taste-testers. You will find infinitely more contentment and joy when you embrace your likes instead of changing yourself to fit the likes of someone else.

RIGHT NOW REMINDER:

God has given you passions, preferences, and loves. Embrace them instead of changing them for someone else, and you will find joy in what you like.

LOOK FOR THE FRUIT

*But the Spirit produces love, joy,
peace, patience, kindness, goodness,
faithfulness, humility, and self-control.
There is no law against such things as these.
And those who belong to Christ Jesus
have put to death their human nature
with all its passions and desires.
The Spirit has given us life;
He must also control our lives.*
GALATIANS 5:22–25 GNT

We'd all love to be more joyous, peaceful, humble, and good. But, try as we might, it's difficult to will ourselves to display these qualities in our day-to-day lives. We get tired and cranky, we say something flippant we regret, and we boast in our accomplishments in order to gain favor in the eyes of others. It's plain that we cannot "will" ourselves to be more loving, more patient, more self-controlled. But if we root our desires in the Spirit, bringing our wants and needs to God to be released, realigned, and restored, we can display the fruit of the Spirit. As we come to the Holy Spirit in prayer more and more, we can look for the fruits mentioned in today's verse blossoming in us.

The bitter fruit of a life out of sync with God is selfishness, pride, and angst. And when we allow our desire for a romantic relationship to be rooted in this human nature, we will only experience these sour and disappointing fruits. But, we find hope and restoration in a life rooted instead in the Holy Spirit. The more time you spend with God, the more the fruit of the Spirit will blossom in you. The more the Holy Spirit works within you, the more you will find the peace, goodness, and self-control you long for, even in your feelings about singleness. We can't manufacture the fruit of the Spirit on our own, but we can surrender to God and watch Him redeem our lives. The Spirit has given us life!

RIGHT NOW REMINDER:

Look for the fruit in your own life.
Is it the fruit of human nature
or the fruit of the Spirit?

WHETHER YOU FEEL CONTENT IN YOUR SINGLENESS OR A DEEP SENSE OF LONGING FOR A RELATIONSHIP, YOU WON'T BE TRULY AT PEACE IN YOUR RIGHT NOW UNTIL YOU BRING THOSE FEELINGS TO GOD.

NOT A PLAN B

I will instruct you and teach you
in the way you should go;
I will counsel you with my eye upon you.
PSALM 32:8 ESV

Life doesn't often go as expected. As a single woman, you know that to be true. You lose a job you loved due to a global pandemic, you move to a new city and it's not as great as you imagined, you struggle with money and budgeting more than you ever thought you would. And your singleness, in one way or another, was probably pretty unexpected too.

Maybe you thought you'd be married with kids and a dog by now, maybe you wanted to try out the dating scene but you aren't finding a lot of prospects. Or maybe you just thought your season as a single woman wouldn't last this long. Because of this, your single life might feel like your plan B scenario. Like if all else fails, if you don't meet someone, if you don't get married, if you don't have kids, your back-up plan is to try and be happily single. The danger here is that if you view your single life as a plan B, you'll never be content with your life today because you'll view it as a lesser-than option. But just because things didn't go as you originally planned does not mean you are missing out on a better version of your life—your plan A.

Singleness, and where you find yourself today, is not a plan B scenario. Nothing has gone wrong in your life to cause you to have to move from a plan A to a plan B. You are living God's plan A for your life right now! As Psalm 32:8 explains, God has ordained this "plan A" life for you. He knows this is the "way you should go." Just because you might not have expected your singleness, God is not surprised, worried, or confused. His eye is upon you. He is executing His magnificent plan for your life today.

RIGHT NOW REMINDER:

Singleness is not a plan B life—
it's today's plan A.

TAMING THE TONGUE

With the tongue we praise our Lord and Father,
and with it we curse human beings,
who have been made in God's likeness.
Out of the same mouth come praise and cursing.
My brothers and sisters, this should not be.
Can both fresh water and salt water flow
from the same spring? My brothers and sisters,
can a fig tree bear olives, or a grapevine bear figs?
Neither can a salt spring produce fresh water.
JAMES 3:9–12 NIV

We've all said some things we regret. Maybe once you were trying to be funny around new friends and said something cutting at the expense of another. Maybe your jealousy of a coworker or classmate prompted some pretty harsh slander, which you felt bad about right after it came out of your mouth. Or maybe your feelings about singleness catch you spreading gossip about other people's relationships, in hopes that it will make you feel better about your lack of one.

Taming our tongue, and therefore regretting what comes out of our mouth less often, is a hard thing to do, but we don't have to do it alone.

Today's passage reminds us to tame our tongues in order to live more holy, God-centered lives.

The thing about taming the tongue is, we can't do it on our own. We can't will ourselves to speak less harshly to others, talk more positively of others, or gossip less. It is only through the work of the Spirit in us that our tongue can be tamed. If we pray to God for help in transforming our speech, He will do it. The Holy Spirit will convict but never condemn, in order to help you to use your tongue more for blessing than for cursing (see Romans 8:1–2). And as single women, when we transform the way we talk about others, whether they are in relationships or not, our hearts and our minds will be impacted for good, freeing us from regret.

RIGHT NOW REMINDER:

*The Holy Spirit is at work within you
to help you tame your tongue.
Ask Him to prompt and guide you today.*

CHRISTIAN DATING

Don't become partners with those who reject God. How can you make a partnership out of right and wrong? That's not partnership; that's war. Is light best friends with dark? Does Christ go strolling with the Devil? Do trust and mistrust hold hands? Who would think of setting up pagan idols in God's holy Temple? But that is exactly what we are, each of us a temple in whom God lives.

II CORINTHIANS 6:14–16 THE MESSAGE

Have you ever tried online dating? If so, you know the simultaneous thrilling and nerve-racking reality of swiping through men to find someone you might have a connection with. It's hard to narrow down what you're looking for on these apps. Maybe you want someone who lives close, someone in a similar profession or life stage, or someone who has similar hobbies. Maybe you're looking for someone who makes you laugh, who exhibits patience, or who is cool under pressure. The pool of potentials seems to grow smaller and smaller with each preference, with each swipe, and God's Word reminds us of the most important preference of all: that we date someone who has a relationship with God. God desires a loving relationship for you that draws you nearer to Him.

As today's passage states, we are called to avoid dating those who don't share our beliefs. But this can be a really hard truth to accept. Especially as a single woman who so longs for a relationship, rejecting kind, respectful, fun guys on the basis of their faith seems unnecessarily harsh. However, if you've had personal experiences dating both guys who share your faith and those who don't, you know what a difference it makes. The right person will encourage your faith to grow and will point you back to Christ in all that they do. They will pray with you, talk to you about God, and be open about their own relationship with Him. The right person encourages you to grow closer to God instead of distracting you from Him and pulling you away.

RIGHT NOW REMINDER:

God has called you to date someone who will grow your faith and point you back to Christ.

CHANGES

On a good day, enjoy yourself;
On a bad day, examine your conscience.
God arranges for both kinds of days
so that we won't take anything for granted.
ECCLESIASTES 7:14 THE MESSAGE

The Greek philosopher Heraclitus is quoted as saying, "The only constant in life is change." And even though you probably haven't changed your last name or your marital status at this point in life, you know this to be true. No matter how old you are, your life has already undergone numerous changes. You might have moved across the state or across the country, changed majors, schools, or jobs, or just started to enjoy the poached eggs or kale salad you wouldn't touch as a kid. We constantly change our clothes, our likes and dislikes, and our minds. And while many of us will eventually change our marital status, not all of us will.

Marriage isn't a necessary change you need to undergo—like learning to tie your shoes, do your laundry, or pay your bills. Marriage is a blessing for many, as well as a huge life change, but it is not a promise for all of us. Instead of letting that thought discourage you, may it bring you a sense of relief and a sense of peace. Release yourself from the pressure that you need to get married in order to check a box, be taken seriously, or advance into adulthood.

Your life will be full of unexpected blessings and messy and beautiful changes, whether you stay single forever or eventually get married. And we can be sure that our lives will be characterized by change, but we can't be sure one of these changes will be to our relationship status. And that's okay, because marriage is a possible life-change, not a vital or mandatory one. No matter what changes await you in this crazy life, you can rest assured that God is watching over you. He knows each and every single change that will take place in your time here on earth. Rest easy in His steadfastness amidst the changes.

RIGHT NOW REMINDER:

Marriage isn't a necessary change you need to check off in order to live a fuller, more meaningful life.

GOD OF OUR TIME

But I trust in you, O Lord; I say,
"You are my God.
My times are in your hand."
PSALM 31:14-15 ESV

It often feels like there's not enough time in the day. We might feel the expectations of work or school along with running errands, working out, cooking meals, seeing friends, setting aside time to spend with Jesus, and getting a good night's sleep. Phew! It's just too much. And when we feel like we have too much on our plate, it can put our soul in to a state of hurry – rushing from one thing to the next, quickly accomplishing task after task. You might even be so accustomed to this flurry that you don't even notice how fast you're moving. You cook dinner quickly, try to fall asleep as fast as possible, or answer emails at red lights because you just don't have the time.

Take a deep breath. Today, we can slow down and learn from the pace our Savior Jesus set in His ministry. You see, Jesus was not in a hurry. He did not rush from one place to another, but He kept His eyes open for opportunities to heal, encourage, and teach. He knew that lives were changed not only when He arrived at a destination, but in encounters along the journey as well. Jesus was intentional with His time, but He did not hold it tightly. Like Him, we can slow down and move from task to task with more intention, both checking in with ourselves and with the world around us on the way. Because when it comes right down to it, we are not in charge of time. We will never master it, harness it, or have power over it. Our Lord is also Lord over our time. So we can slow down, cease rushing, and experience the journey. There will be time to do what you need to do. Follow the rhythms of Jesus: slow, purposeful, and mindful over His time.

RIGHT NOW REMINDER:

We will never lord over our time,
and that's good news.
It allows us to slow down,
take some pressure off,
and experience the journey of life.

LIVING IN THE NOW

I pray that God, the source of hope,
will fill you completely with joy and peace
because you trust in Him.
Then you will overflow with confident hope
through the power of the Holy Spirit.
ROMANS 15:13 NLT

You're probably putting off some things until you get married. You might be delaying big life purchases like buying a new car, going on an international vacation, or purchasing a house all your own. Or you could be putting off small but necessary updates: new pots and pans that actually have matching lids, a fancy but pricey coffee maker, a new couch to replace your worn and lumpy one. Logically, it seems to make sense: you don't want to commit to anything prematurely, especially if you have hopes you'll be making important decisions alongside a spouse sooner rather than later. The thing is, whether we delay small or big changes and purchases, we aren't living our lives to the fullest right now. We are living for the future instead of enjoying today.

Don't delay your joy, your life, just because you

may get married in the future. Live today in the here and now, and you won't only find contentment, you'll "overflow with confident hope through the power of the Holy Spirit." Living your life, enjoying what you enjoy, embracing your days as they are right now is an exercise in joy and in trust. When you live as if you're delaying life until marriage, you are putting all the pressure on yourself, as if this will dictate your likelihood of a relationship. Conversely, if you take advantage of the season you're in now and find joy in it, you are placing your trust in God for today, tomorrow, and many seasons to come. So buy that new car, upgrade your living room, or purchase a full matching set of silverware for your kitchen. The time for living in the fullness of God is now.

RIGHT NOW REMINDER:

God is your source of hope, joy, and peace.
When you really live out of the current season of life,
your trust in Him will grow.

CHOO/ING JOY

Rejoice in the Lord always:
and again I say, Rejoice.
PHILIPPIANS 4:4 KJV

While you're single, you'll probably go through a period of time when you don't want to look for the good. You're over it. You don't want to recognize the gifts this season has given you, the unique blessings of this moment in time. Your focus on what you think you lack overtakes all of that—you are tired of striving to see the positives when in reality, your heart is downcast. While it's okay to feel sad or angry from time to time about your circumstance, trouble comes when these feelings morph from being an ebb and flow into a solid immoveable force called bitterness. Bitterness stems from a feeling that you are being treated unfairly or unjustly, and it can sour you toward those around you who have what you want. Bitterness eats away at your flourishing relationships and can turn you against others, including yourself. It can also sour you toward God when you feel as though He isn't giving you what you think you deserve—namely a romantic relationship on your preferred timetable. When we allow bitterness to settle into our souls, it affects our relationships, our perspective, and our day-to-day life. But the antidote to bitterness is choosing joy.

Choosing joy is hard work. That's because it's a conscious choice you have to make, to turn from bitterness and choose to see the goodness around us. Simply put, it's a decision. And when you choose to ground your joy in the Lord, it will abound all the more. Joy doesn't have to come from exciting events, big life changes, or colossal personal wins. You can choose to have joy in the daily grind of your job, in the imperfect place you call home, even in your homemade lunch of leftovers. You can choose to see joy when people continually ask about your dating life, when you see another coworker get engaged, or when you get a friend's save-the-date in the mail. The more you choose to see moments of joy, the more any bitterness that may be in your heart will deflect and fade. No matter your relationship status, choosing joy will shift your perspective and root you in the goodness of God.

RIGHT NOW REMINDER:

We can choose joy over bitterness,
no matter what our relationship status is.

KEEP AT IT

Consider it a great joy, my brothers and sisters,
whenever you experience various trials,
because you know that the testing
of your faith produces endurance.
And let endurance have its full effect,
so that you may be mature
and complete, lacking nothing.
JAMES 1:1–4 CSB

Don't give up on God because you feel like your prayers haven't been answered. Even when you feel like you can't wait any longer—as though your cries for a relationship are bouncing off the ceiling and your loneliness is going unaccounted for. Even when your desire for a relationship feels like an all-consuming thought that you're not sure God is even there. Take heart, because He is. Keep waiting, keep hoping, and keep praying. The trials that singleness brings will come and go, but through them all, God is cultivating a spirit of courage, of tenacity, and of perseverance within you. Hold on to hope, because God has heard every single one of your prayers, and He will continue hearing, answering, and loving you through it all.

You've seen God answer prayers before, whether in your own life or through the testimony of someone else. Those testimonies—of people healed, of ordained moves or job changes, of relationships restored—are living proof that holding on to hope in the midst of a hard season is worth it. Keep at it. As you keep waiting and hoping and praying for a relationship, God will continue to teach you, shape you, and draw you closer to Himself. As you plant seeds for tomorrow, God is not ignoring you or turning a deaf ear to your pleas, He is pruning your heart. He is developing endurance within you while you wait for His plan to be revealed. God is continually refining you, developing you into a more mature and complete version of yourself. God will never give up on you, so don't you give up either.

RIGHT NOW REMINDER:

If you've been waiting for an answer to your prayers about your singleness for a long time, do not lose hope. Keeping praying, keep waiting, keep drawing closer to Him.

EVEN WHEN YOU FEEL LIKE YOU'VE BEEN WAITING FOR A REALLY LONG TIME, KEEP WAITING, KEEP HOPING, AND KEEP PRAYING. THE TRIALS THAT SINGLENESS BRINGS WILL COME AND GO, BUT THROUGH THEM GOD IS CULTIVATING A SPIRIT OF COURAGE, OF TENACITY, AND OF PERSEVERANCE WITHIN YOU.

YOU Be YOU

For am I now seeking the approval of man, or of God?
Or am I trying to please man?
If I were still trying to please man,
I would not be a servant of Christ.
GALATIANS 1:10 ESV

You are allowed to decide how you want to live your life, which can be challenging because, as a single woman, you'll get all sorts of questions, advice, assumptions, and comments thrown at you. Some people might be impressed that you are happily single, some might pressure you into dating any number of random single men they know, and some might be envious of the freedom and flexibility this season affords you. It's sometimes hard to separate yourself from the noise. But it's really important to decide how *you* feel about your singleness.

Come to God, block out all the interfering clamor, and search your own heart. How do you feel about being single? You might think you long for a relationship, only to realize you just long for the external pressure from others to be silenced. You might realize you'd prefer to start dating in a few years, after you're established in your career or you've had time to travel. Or you might discover you do want a relationship, but not because it's the assumed thing to do but because you would love a companion to go through life with. If we don't take time with ourselves and with God, asking after our own relationship status, we can get swept up in the current of outside pressure. It's easier to agree with others that being in a relationship would make your life easier or that you should desire a husband than to decide for yourself and comfortably sit with your own feelings. But, as today's verse explains, we aren't seeking the approval of man but an alignment with God's plan for our lives. So ask God to reveal to you His plan for you in regard to romantic relationships. You might find that you didn't want it as much as others were telling you you should, or that you do want a boyfriend or husband, just not yet. There is no right or wrong answer here; you get to decide how you feel about being single.

RIGHT NOW REMINDER:

Only the approval of God matters.
Search your heart to discover how you feel
about your singleness, and then allow yourself
to feel content with the answer.

YOU ARE IMPORTANT

You are the light of the world.
A city situated on a hill cannot be hidden.
No one lights a lamp and puts it under a basket,
but rather on a lampstand, and it gives light
for all who are in the house. In the same way,
let your light shine before others,
so that they may see your good works
and give glory to your Father in heaven.
MATTHEW 5:14–16 CSB

You are of immense value to God as you are, right now. God created you with unique talents, gifts, and personality traits for a reason, and He loves who you are. You are important to Him. Your value doesn't decrease because you aren't in a relationship or increase once you walk down the aisle, own a house, or have kids. In fact, your value has nothing to do with your relationship status or your accomplishments. Today's passage doesn't include any caveats like "if you are married, you are the light of the world" or "if you've had a lot of dating experience, you should let your light shine before others." It sounds silly when you put it like that, but we often equate our importance and our value with our accomplishments and our relationships, including romantic relationships.

God calls you "the light of the world" because you are important to Him just as you are right now. He desires for you to be yourself—in personality, in your likes and dislikes, in your hobbies, and in your career—and to show off the glory of God in you. You can be that shining light, set up for those around you to see, as you are right now. Your love for God and for others will give glory to Him. As you accept this truth, may you be empowered by God to be who you were created to be, single and not sorry.

RIGHT NOW REMINDER:

You are important,
just as you are right now.

REST EASY

Those who live in the shelter of the Most High
will find rest in the shadow of the Almighty.
This I declare about the LORD: He alone is my refuge,
my place of safety; He is my God, and I trust Him.
PSALM 91:1–2 NLT

As single women, sometimes we get stuck running on the hamster wheel of striving. We strive to always look put together when we leave our house—just in case we see someone cute out and about. We strive to act just the right amount of bubbly, just the perfect amount of sassy and well-spoken, in order to convince others that we are worthy of love and that we are fun to be around. We strive to field questions about our singleness with grace and a collected chillness, never admitting how we really feel. Sounds easy, right? The thing is, striving is really, really tiring. And if we strive to date, get married, and end our singleness instead of aligning with God's timing, we'll just end up exhausted, defeated, and upset. What if we got off the hamster wheel and instead learned to rest in the shelter of the Most High?

Striving stems from feeling as though we are never doing enough—we haven't used our time wisely, we think that if only we did this one more thing, circumstances will change, or we can't catch up to where society says we should be. Instead, we can end the exhausting routine of striving and find rest in God. God's desire for us is to come to Him and rest instead of ramping up our expectations of ourselves because we are striving to meet the world's standards. When we trust God, He is our place of safety, our refuge. And when we feel safe, we can rest easy.

You don't have to worry that you're falling behind, you've done something wrong, or you've disappointed others. When you deepen your relationship with God, you can live each day knowing that you are safe and loved. You can rest. As Augustine said, "Our hearts are restless until they rest in You."

RIGHT NOW REMINDER:

*Cease striving and
release yourself to the rest of God.
He is your refuge and your place of safety.*

ON STUDYING THE BIBLE

All Scripture is inspired by God and is useful to teach us what is true and to make us realize what is wrong in our lives. It corrects us when we are wrong and teaches us to do what is right. God uses it to prepare and equip His people to do every good work.

II TIMOTHY 3:16–17 NLT

If you grew up in the eighties or nineties, you are probably very familiar with the term "stranger danger." This term permeated the culture and taught us as kids not to engage with strangers because they couldn't be trusted. Don't take anything a stranger offers you, don't chat with them even if they seem friendly, and definitely don't accept any rides from them. The idea is, we can't trust someone we don't know. And while useful when it comes to a stranger at the grocery store or a chatty but kinda creepy neighbor, this line of thinking can be detrimental when it comes to your relationship with God and studying the Bible. Because, if you don't study the Word of God, you won't get to know who God is. And if you don't know who God is, how can you trust Him? We study the Bible to learn about God's character and to learn how to entrust ourselves more fully to Him.

As single women, we have more time than most other seasons to commit to studying the Bible and growing our relationship with God. It can be overwhelming to begin a two-thousand-plus-page Bible, but if we reframe it as His own love letter to us and an opportunity to understand Him better, it's exciting! God has given us all the tools we need to understand His Word, and we can be empowered by that truth.

You are not too young; you are not too old. You are not under-educated; you do not have too many questions. You can understand the Bible, and you can see it transform your life. You are a smart, capable, Spirit-led woman. As you study His Word more, you will learn to trust God in new and deep ways, drawing yourself closer to Him than you ever thought possible.

RIGHT NOW REMINDER:

You are a smart, capable, empowered woman.
You have all the tools you need to understand the Bible
and to deepen your relationship with God.

ETERNALLY MINDED

So if you have been raised with Christ, seek the things
above, where Christ is, seated at the right hand of God.
Set your minds on things above, not on earthly things.
For you died, and your life is hidden with Christ in God.
When Christ, who is your life, appears,
then you also will appear with him in glory.

COLOSSIANS 3:1–4 CSB

How will I make it through another wedding with no plus one?

Why do I have to do all of these errands and solve all of these issues on my own?

Who will I find out there in this great big world?

When will I stop feeling lonely?

These are all big, weighty questions—ones you've probably asked at some point in your life as a single woman. But when we get bogged down in the questions of how/why/who/when, our focus shifts off Christ and onto the myriad of issues in our day-to-day lives. This is where an eternal mindset comes in to restore us, energize us, and give us hope. An eternal mindset is a reframing of our days, a reminder that this life here on earth is short in comparison to the eternity we will spend with God in heaven. When we focus on the finiteness of our lives, roughly eighty to ninety years, we realize that the only thing that matters is God—knowing God, studying God, and telling others about God. As citizens of heaven (see Philippians 3:20), we are just visitors here on earth. We can soak in this truth, allowing it to empower us to live a life that brings God glory here while we wait to go to heaven.

Singleness is hard. But singleness won't break you. And if you "set your mind on things above," remembering that you will one day be with God in glory, you'll find the burden of singleness to be lighter. An eternal mindset helps us to anchor our lives here and now more deeply in Christ, numbering our days accordingly (see Psalm 90:12). As David Jeremiah says, "Don't let obstacles along the road to eternity shake your confidence in God's promise. The Holy Spirit is God's seal that you will arrive. "

RIGHT NOW REMINDER:

With an eternal mindset,
you will be empowered to live freely today.
Your citizenship is in heaven.

AFRAID OF THE DARK

In peace I will lie down and sleep,
for you alone, Lord, make me dwell in safety.
PSALM 4:8 NIV

Were you ever afraid of the dark? As kids, our imaginations run wild as to what could be behind that sheet of blackness that envelops us when the sun goes down and the lights go off. If you suffered from darkness-induced panic when you were younger, you probably had some sort of coping mechanism or solution to calm you down. Maybe it was a bright night-light, a treasured stuffed animal, or a calming noise machine. We needed these tools to help soothe our fears of the dark and remind us that even though it might be the dead of the night, we weren't alone. Even if we couldn't see what was going on around us, we were okay. We were safe, as long as we saw the star-shaped night-light, hugged our teddy tight, or listened to the sounds of a summer night on loop.

A big desire for many of us as single women is to have a companion, someone to do life with. We want someone to watch a favorite TV show with, to cook a new recipe with, or to talk through the everyday ups and downs of life with. The ultimate fear here is similar to our childhood fear of the dark, that left alone, we are not safe or cared for. We need to know we are going to be okay. And, as today's verse reminds us, God is our safety and our reassurance. We can go throughout our days with the peace of Christ, knowing that we have someone to do life with right now—God. We can lie down in this same peace and sleep soundly, knowing God is always with us and always watching out for us. We don't need to be afraid of the areas of our lives that look dark and hazy, unclear to our eyes and a little scary. We have God, our light in the darkness, our comfort, and our reassurance right there with us.

RIGHT NOW REMINDER:

God is your safe place.

DEBORAH

Has not the LORD gone ahead of you?

The story of Deborah in Judges 4–5 serves as a great reminder that there are God-empowered women in leadership—both single and married—who are breaking cultural norms. Women who lived around the time of Deborah were most often valued or honored in relation to their husband's standing, and culturally they had very few rights. Today's comparison would be the inherent value of married women over single, making us single women feel less than. Deborah stood in juxtaposition to her cultural norm, serving Israel not only as a judge but also a warrior, poet, and prophet. Judges 4:4–5 says: "Now Deborah, a prophet, the wife of Lappidoth, was leading Israel at that time. She held court under the Palm of Deborah between Ramah and Bethel in the hill country of Ephraim, and the Israelites went up to her to have their disputes decided" (NIV). We can take inspiration from her to align ourselves with the purposes of God, even if they feel bold and brave, trusting that He has our best in mind.

It would have been shocking for early Christian readers that it was not Deborah's relationship to her husband that proved significant in her story but her command over Israel and their trust in her. In fact, the phrase "wife of Lappidoth" could be translated "woman of fire," which says more about Deborah's character than her marriage relationship. You are also a woman of fire, a God-empowered woman who does not need to allow your relationship status to define you. From the beginning of Deborah's story, the text demonstrates a clear difference in the inherent value of women from God's perspective as opposed to the cultural perspective. Although Deborah was married, her relationship status was just a facet of her life. She listened to God's calling in all that she did, leading the Israelite army to victory while relying on Him. As women of fire, we remember Deborah as we go boldly into our lives, listening to God's calling instead of the cultural messages that surround us.

RIGHT NOW REMINDER:

You are a strong, fierce, powerful woman of God.

ATTENTION

For who has stood in the council
of the Lᴏʀᴅ to see and hear His word?
Who has paid attention to His word and obeyed?

JEREMIAH 23:18 CSB

Many of us long for romantic attention: getting dressed up in our best outfit for a date, wanting to hold a new someone's hand, being noticed in a crowd from across the room. As single women, we long for butterflies in our stomach before a date, for rom-com–level devotion, and to be noticed for who we are. But the hard truth is, oftentimes those whom we desire attention from aren't even thinking about us. That boy who does homework at the same coffee shop as you, that cute new coworker you enjoy interacting with, that guy in the same big friend group as you—they might not even notice you. We long for attention, but we are not promised it. So realistically, we waste our time in the longing, waiting for the perfect man to turn our way. While we've been setting our intentions on getting noticed, the whole time God has set His affections on us, and He is waiting to spend time with us. God is there, ready and waiting for you to see the loving attention and affection He has for you here and now.

Have we given consideration to the attention that God gives us, or have we wasted our time longing for attention in all the wrong places? This isn't to say it's wrong to want a relationship, to want kind and affectionate attention in a romantic way. Instead, it's important to be aware that often the attention we seek from others will simply not be found at all times in human relationships. God is there for us, waiting patiently for us to turn our attention to Him. Whenever we seek Him, pray to Him, or look to Him for answers, He is always there. His attention is not fickle or fleeting or unpredictable. He will always turn our way in kindness, empathy, and grace. We simply must humble ourselves enough to realize that we need Him more than we need romantic attention, turning our hearts to Him and finding our home in His grace.

RIGHT NOW REMINDER:

God has set His affections on you and longs to spend time with you.

ROM-COMS
AND FAIRY TALES

Those who trust in the LORD will find new strength.
They will soar high on wings like eagles. They will run
and not grow weary. They will walk and not faint.

ISAIAH 40:31 NLT

Who doesn't love a good fairy tale? Many of us grew up reading stories of princesses being rescued from certain despair by a brave and handsome prince, watching movies of women getting whisked off their feet after catching Prince Charming's eye at a ball, and seeing shows of girls just like us realizing all their dreams came true once they got married. And all these fairy tales end with "and they lived happily ever after . . ."

While reading these stories and watching these magical movies is certainly fun, it's no wonder the message was ingrained in us that to be truly happy, your life should include a flawless whirlwind romance. This is further perpetuated by the rom-coms we moved on to later in life, the meet-cute stories our friends go on about, and the tales of a perfect online dating romance we are told to encourage us to keep at it. But reality varies vastly from most of these stories.

Whether imaginary or real, most of these stories make up an extremely small percentage of the normal person's dating experience and romance.

We need a reminder that pursuing a romantic relationship is not all Instagram-worthy dates, seamless conversation, and clear and obvious attraction. Real life looks a lot more like clunky first dates, halting conversation, and heart-to-hearts about defining the relationship. Dating can of course still be fun and exciting, but we cannot set up a standard in our minds that equates to fairy tales. We must let go of the perfect best-case scenarios and stop waiting to be swept off our feet. When we release the story in our mind, we see that we can live our own happily ever after. If we look to God's plan instead of getting inspiration from rom-coms and fairy tales, we can sink into the promises of God, and there we shall find new strength for whatever lies ahead. When you follow God, your life can be beautiful and joyful, Prince Charming or no.

RIGHT NOW REMINDER:

If you work hard to release the story in your mind of your perfect romance, you are giving yourself grace as you align your heart with God's plan.

THE MERCY OF GOD

What we see now is like a dim image in a mirror; then we shall see face-to-face. What I know now is only partial; then it will be complete— as complete as God's knowledge of me.

I CORINTHIANS 13:12 GNT

God is a good, kind God who wants good things for us. As single women who might long for a relationship, it's comforting to rest in this promise— and in the mercy God gives through it. The mercy of God can be defined as God's tenderhearted love toward us. His mercy is expansive, all-consuming, and so very beautiful, we can't even see the full extent of it here on earth. We don't know how He's working because we can't plainly see His plan. This passage in I Corinthians uses the imagery of a mirror to explain our human view of His plan for our lives—a dim, hazy reflection. But God has the full, clear, beautiful picture. As Thomas Merton wrote, "My life is a mystery which I do not attempt to really understand, as though I were led by the hand in a night where I see nothing but can fully depend on the love and protection of Him who guides me."

We don't know the full scope of what God has protected us from. Maybe you haven't dated much and can't understand why God hasn't put men in your path who will pursue you. Maybe you liked someone and felt that they liked you back, but nothing ever came to fruition. Maybe you dated a guy you could really see yourself falling for, but it ended, and you still aren't sure why. Whatever your circumstance, these hard moments of life and singleness can be reframed: what if God was sparing you from something you couldn't even see? God wants the best for you—in your job, in your community, and in your dating relationships. Because we see His plan only dimly now, we cannot grasp to the full extent how He has worked to protect, nurture, and care for us. Perhaps your singleness is an act of mercy from God.

RIGHT NOW REMINDER:

God loves you and wants good things for you.
Your singleness may be the result of Him
mercifully sparing you from something
that would hurt or harm you.

Because we see his plan only dimly now, we cannot grasp to the full extent how he has worked to protect, nurture, and care for us. Perhaps your singleness is an

ACT OF MERCY FROM GOD.

SHAME BE GONE

There is therefore now no condemnation
for those who are in Christ Jesus.
For the law of the Spirit of life has set you free
in Christ Jesus from the law of sin and death.

ROMANS 8:1–2 ESV

Do you go through your days feeling shame around your singleness? This could look like embarrassment at not being in a romantic relationship, an inkling that you've done something wrong and caused your singleness, or just a general guilt around feeling behind in life. Shame feels icky and clingy, and it weighs us down. Shame takes our eyes off the beauty of our lives as single women and turns us inward to despair. If you feel this way, you need to know this shame is not from God. This feeling that you aren't enough, are half to a whole, or have done something wrong is not what God desires for you. Christine Caine puts it this way, "What a crafty enemy we have. Can you see it? The enemy knows that if he can cause us to hide ourselves—who God made us to be—that it also causes us to lose sight of our identity in God as his image-bearers. Then, because our view of ourselves has been diminished, we shrink from stepping into the destiny God created for us." As today's verse explains, our God is a God who frees us from condemnation, empowering us to live abundant, shame-free days! God wants to set you free from any shame you feel.

Let me say it again: there is no shame in being single. Whether you have a dating history that would take hours to recount or have never had a boyfriend before; whether you desire marriage or not; whether you're surrounded by couples and families or your friends are mostly single; whether you feel outside pressure to date or feel relatively at ease with your dating life—you are free from shame in Christ. Because you have the Spirit that gives life living inside you, you can take pride in your single status, knowing it's where God wants you.

RIGHT NOW REMINDER:

Any shame you feel about your singleness is not from God. He wants to release you from the condemnation that weighs you down and uplift you as you see the freedom and beauty of your life today.

CHASING CONTENTMENT

*Not that I was ever in need, for I have learned
how to be content with whatever I have.
I know how to live on almost nothing or
with everything. I have learned the secret
of living in every situation, whether it is with
a full stomach or empty, with plenty or little.
For I can do everything through Christ,
who gives me strength.*

PHILIPPIANS 4:11–13 NLT

What does it look like to be content while also hoping things will change? Chances are, if you've been single for a while, you've wanted that to change at one time or another. And even if you are pretty satisfied with your singleness right now, there are other areas of your life where you long for a shift. Maybe in your career, your home life, or your finances. Our desire for change in one area of our lives can feel pretty all-consuming at times, taking our focus off any good gifts we've been given. So how do we balance desiring change with pursuing contentment? The secret is found in Christ.

As Paul writes in today's passage, contentment is not realized in our life circumstances, our relationship status, our financial situation, or our career. We can get caught up pursuing the next big goal, the next life event, the next promotion, and feeling as if we are chasing contentment rather than experiencing it. Therefore, if we seek these avenues as our source of happiness, we will be left wanting. However, if we look to Christ for strength, we will *learn* "how to be content with whatever I have."

By praying to Jesus, studying God's Word, and working to align your heart with His plan, contentment eventually works its way in and settles over your spirit. Gratitude breeds contentment, so thanking God for the things you do have in your life will also help. Living a life of contentment is not as hard as it seems for us single women, as we shift our eyes off our need and instead settle upon Christ, who gives us strength in every season.

RIGHT NOW REMINDER:
Christ is our source of strength and contentment.
If you feel unsettled about your singleness,
come to Him today with your need.

MARY'S SIDE OF THE STORY

As Jesus and the disciples continued on their way to Jerusalem, they came to a certain village where a woman named Martha welcomed him into her home. Her sister, Mary, sat at the Lord's feet, listening to what he taught. But Martha was distracted by the big dinner she was preparing. She came to Jesus and said, "Lord, doesn't it seem unfair to you that my sister just sits here while I do all the work? Tell her to come and help me."

But the Lord said to her, "My dear Martha, you are worried and upset over all these details! There is only one thing worth being concerned about. Mary has discovered it, and it will not be taken away from her."

LUKE 10:38–42 NLT

The story of Mary and Martha has been used in dozens of sermons, books, and devotionals. Many scholars believe that the Mary spoken about here was Mary Magdalene, who became a faithful disciple of Jesus after He cast seven demons out of her (see Luke 8). Because of this, Mary was not just a woman who sat quietly at Jesus' feet, her testimony included a life formerly possessed by demons and ruled by prostitution. Following Jesus and listening to His teaching had completely turned her life around! Therefore, she knew the importance of sitting near Him and absorbing everything He had to say. Usually Mary's faithfulness to Jesus and His teaching is elevated above the distracted service of her sister Martha, and that's because we can learn from Mary's priorities.

What would it look like to pattern our devotion to Jesus after Mary? While there were many other things to do, Mary prioritized her faith over them all. She even broke cultural norms of hospitality in order to spend time with Christ. As single women with busy lives, we can let our distractions and desires get in the way of our relationship with Jesus. May we instead look to Him first, as everything else falls into to place around us.

RIGHT NOW REMINDER:

Mary's relationship with Jesus was her first priority. What would it look like for us to readjust our priorities to align them with God?

MARTHA'S SIDE OF THE STORY

Martha was upset over all the work she had to do, so she came and said, "Lord, don't you care that my sister has left me to do all the work by myself? Tell her to come and help me!" The Lord answered her, "Martha, Martha! You are worried and troubled over so many things, but just one is needed. Mary has chosen the right thing, and it will not be taken away from her."

LUKE 10:40–42 GNT

Mary and Martha are not enemies but sisters representing the love of God. As we read in the previous devotion, Mary did prioritize learning from Jesus over her household duties, which allowed her to grow in her faith. However, this does not mean that Martha was in the wrong. Martha actually did what was culturally appropriate and acceptable at the time, as their culture valued hospitality and service to guests. Hospitality is also a core component of the kingdom of God, and Martha was embodying that here on earth. Jesus' rebuke of Martha is full of love and compassion, as He sees that Martha is demonstrating her love for Him through active service. He doesn't tell her that what she is doing is wrong but that there are more important opportunities at hand.

In this story, Mary is representing a dedication and commitment to Jesus over everything, and Martha demonstrates a kingdom hospitality. Both are important to embody as followers of Christ. Martha's side of the story reminds us that, in everything we do, we can honor Christ. It also reminds us that even these good, God-honoring things can distract us from our real source of peace—Jesus. Similarly, the pursuit of a dating relationship or the desire to be married is good and God-honoring. However, if we get too wrapped up in them, we can get distracted from the true source of our hope and joy, Jesus Christ Himself.

RIGHT NOW REMINDER:

Martha is not the villain of the story, and neither are you. It's right and good to want to please God, but we can align these desires under the priority of growing in our relationship with Jesus.

HEALING

We are often troubled, but not crushed;
sometimes in doubt, but never in despair;
there are many enemies,
but we are never without a friend;
and though badly hurt at times,
we are not destroyed.

II CORINTHIANS 4:8–9 GNT

We all have pasts, hurts, and parts of ourselves we'd rather not examine. It's hard, deep work to get to know ourselves and to confront these traumas—why we act the way we do, how we can mend our hearts, and what it means for us to look like a more healed and whole version of ourselves. As a single woman, now is the time to get to know yourself at this deepest level, to heal and to thrive. And as you get to know yourself more deeply, you naturally rebuild and open up to God and others in new ways. Psalm 139:13 says, "You created every part of me; you put me together in my mother's womb." God created you in a beautiful complexity, and He desires for you to live a healed, free, magnificent life.

Throughout our lives, we will continually heal and work through our past hurts in order to become a more whole version of ourselves. As we grow and change, we are constantly discovering new things about ourselves. And healing looks different for everyone. For many of us, it will look like therapy with a mental health professional. It can also look like journaling, asking yourself hard questions, and dedicating time to a lot of prayer. Yes, tackling your past can be scary, but the abundant life you'll discover as you heal is more beautiful than you can imagine. Now is the time to learn who you really are—not because you want to be the perfect version of yourself for someone else but because God desires for you to know your "inward parts" as He does, for you to get to know yourself as you get to know God more deeply.

RIGHT NOW REMINDER:

Healing the deepest parts of you
is a difficult but beautiful path.
You are never alone on this journey;
God is with you every step of the way.

YOUR VOICE MATTERS

Let the message about Christ, in all its richness,
fill your lives. Teach and counsel each other
with all the wisdom He gives. Sing psalms and hymns
and spiritual songs to God with thankful hearts.

COLOSSIANS 3:16 NLT

What you have to say matters. Your unique passions, gifts, and talents all manifest themselves in speech at some point and influences others. But sometimes we are our own worst enemies, inwardly coming up with a list of reasons why we shouldn't speak up, lead, teach, or counsel others. And as single women, we can use our singleness as yet another excuse. If we use our singleness as a crutch, we can't step into the power that God has created within each of us. We each have been given the power to encourage and uplift those around us as we let the message of Christ fill our lives. Believing and living out the truth that your voice matters will change your life.

When you believe that your voice matters, you become more in tune with the Holy Spirit living inside you, who will guide you as you interact with people on a day-to-day basis. The teaching and counseling talked about in today's verse doesn't have to be on a grand scale, on a stage in front of thousands of people, starting a popular podcast, or becoming a social media influencer. It could look more like talking to that woman in the grocery store or listening to your friend who's going through a hard time. You interact with people every day who might need a word from you, whether encouragement, advice, or comfort. Believing that your voice matters empowers you to use it to support others. And whether you've been gifted as a teacher, a writer, a speaker, an encourager, or a great source of advice, God loves when you use your voice to help others and to bring them closer to Him.

RIGHT NOW REMINDER:

The Holy Spirit is working inside you, and what you have to say matters. Your unique voice matters. Use it.

IF WE USE OUR SINGLENESS **AS A CRUTCH,** WE CAN'T STEP INTO THE POWER THAT GOD HAS CREATED WITHIN EACH OF US. WE EACH HAVE BEEN GIVEN INFLUENCE BY GOD, THE POWER TO **ENCOURAGE AND UPLIFT** THOSE AROUND US, AS WE LET THE MESSAGE OF CHRIST FILL OUR LIVES.

NEVER ALONE

Don't be afraid, for I am with you.
Don't be discouraged, for I am your God.
I will strengthen you and help you.
I will hold you up with my victorious right hand.
ISAIAH 41:10 NLT

Sometimes it's hard to resist the lie that romance is happening for everyone but you. All your friends are getting the male attention you'd like, finding their person in unexpected ways, and falling in love. Meanwhile, you might find yourself the fifth wheel at a dinner, the odd one out at parties, or the one who can't seem to catch a guy's eye. It is downright upsetting to feel like you are being passed over, and in these moments it's hard not to doubt your worth. Your season of singleness, no matter how long it lasts, will involve some highs and some lows, and that's okay. It's learning how to process your way through these times that makes all the difference. When you feel disheartened, and when you take those feelings to God, you are reminded that you are never alone. You are not being passed over, and you are not being forgotten.

While we aren't promised that singleness will be

easy, we are promised that God will be with us when we feel like everyone has found love but us. He will be there when we feel like no one else is. It's the difference between being home alone on a dark, stormy night when the power goes out versus having a great friend there with you. The circumstances don't change, but our experience of them does. When we feel that ache of loneliness fill our heart or that soundtrack of lies that we are alone consume our thoughts, we can turn to God, who is there to weather the storm alongside us. When we feel upset, when a storm of emotions swirls within, or when we feel as though we don't know where to turn with our feelings over singleness, God is always there. He is that great friend we need. And knowing and accepting that we are never alone can encourage us, fill us, and strengthen us when we feel like we might be the last single girl on the planet. God is with us.

RIGHT NOW REMINDER:

You are not alone. God is with you to weather whatever storms this season of life brings.

FIND YOUR HOBBY

Whether you eat or drink or whatever you do,
do it all for the glory of God.
I CORINTHIANS 10:31 NIV

What makes you feel alive? Is it when you round the tree-lined corner after a hard hike and finally see that breathtaking view? Do you cherish that art piece you labored over for weeks to create? What about racing through a newly released page-turner while wrapped in a cozy blanket? One of the great gifts of singleness is the time to find a hobby that is perfect for you. When you find it, you feel that spark, knowing this form of self-expression was made for you. Now, I know what you're thinking. I didn't think I had time to cultivate a hobby either. But the more I prioritized downtime to experiment with different hobbies, the more I felt my soul come alive.

Hobbies can be sacred because they connect you with your innermost self: your passions, your desires, your creativity, and your gifts. Therefore, your time cultivating your craft will naturally overflow into a soul connection with your Creator. God is glorified in you when you find a way to connect with yourself and with Him that is fun and free. So try all sorts of hobbies. Maybe you'll find you like something more athletic like trail running, tennis, or kayaking. Maybe you'll discover you can lose yourself in a pottery class or an oil painting. Maybe you'll surprise even yourself with your love for animals, for writing, or for interior design. As today's verse states, whatever you find to do, frame it as an opportunity to connect in a deeper way with yourself and with God. Your hobby can bring you joy and bring your God glory! As single women, we have the opportunity and the free time to try different hobbies and to flourish in this practice. Find out what makes you feel alive. Pull out some new recipes, lace up those tennis shoes, or break out that hammer and electric drill—it's time to create!

RIGHT NOW REMINDER:

You were uniquely created with gifts and talents. Finding a hobby while you're single that you enjoy will connect you to yourself and to God in a new and fun way. You got this.

BODY ReƧPECT

For we are God's masterpiece.
He has created us anew in Christ Jesus,
so we can do the good things
he planned for us long ago.
EPHESIANS 2:10 NLT

There is a self-love movement on the rise that echoes empowering messages such as "love your body," "your weight does not equal your worth," and "your body is good." And it's immensely exciting to see women all over the world love their bodies as God created them, affirming all of these sentiments and more. But for some of us, years of beating up our bodies for what they do or don't look like, obsessing over what they lack, or despising them in comparison to others has made the move to self-love seem near impossible. And as a single woman, your body may be the first place you turn when you are feeling bad about your singleness—a source of blame or lament. If looking at your body positively and treating it with love feels unreachable right now, that's okay. Body respect is here for you today.

Body respect means treating your body with kindness physically, mentally, emotionally, and spiritually while you learn more about it and honor what it needs. This looks like honoring your hunger cues by eating healthy, being kind to your mind through positive thinking, and listening to and responding to your emotions with grace. It also looks like working in tandem with God to identify all the amazing things about your body: how fast your legs can run the grassy path behind your house, how well your eyes can see the beauty of the nearby ocean, how delightful it is to celebrate your friend's birthday over cake and ice cream. God desires for you to respect yourself. And as you grow to respect yourself, you will teach others to respect you as well. God calls you beautiful, cherished, a work of art. You are His masterpiece, your body included. But if those truths feel out of reach for you after years of hating on your body, take a step today toward respecting God in You, the body He's given you, and all the amazing places it will take you in this season.

RIGHT NOW REMINDER:

God created you as an embodied person
and calls you His masterpiece.
How can you move toward body respect today?

ADVOCATE FOR YOURSELF

Therefore, as God's chosen people,
holy and dearly loved, clothe yourselves
with compassion, kindness, humility,
gentleness and patience.
COLOSSIANS 3:12 NIV

Sometimes, in order to appear sweeter or kinder, we let little things slide. You hate pickles and asked for them to be left off, but your sandwich came with them anyway. You really need a few hours alone in between a busy workday and plans with your neighbors, but then your phone rings. Your friend picks you up and her car is boiling hot, but you sweat in silence.

We let everyday inconveniences or preferences like these slide because we think it will make us a better friend, a kinder stranger, and maybe even a better future mate. We might even think that having opinions or desires contrary to others is what is keeping us single. But the reality is that asking for what we want, both in big ways and small, is incredibly empowering. You will learn more by asserting your preferences when it feels slightly awkward than staying silent and feeling uncomfortable or uncared for. Advocating for yourself does not stand in opposition to being kind, respectful, and loving toward others but rather works alongside. You can speak up for what you want and need, knowing that you are emboldened by God.

So ask for what you want. It isn't rude to clarify what you ordered, tell your neighbors you need an hour alone, or ask to adjust the air conditioner. Chances are, the other person won't even think twice about it. When you take these small opportunities to ask for what you want, you are caring for and empowering yourself. And as God's beloved, when you look at the world through the lens of compassion, kindness, humility, gentleness, and patience, you can advocate for yourself and also be a light to the world (see Matthew 5:14–16). Don't be afraid to speak up for what you want, need, or desire.

RIGHT NOW REMINDER:

God has empowered you in boldness.
You can advocate for yourself
and still be humble and kind.

ON FRIENDSHIP WITH FAMILIES

As iron sharpens iron,
so a friend sharpens a friend.
PROVERBS 27:17 NLT

Having friends at various life stages is a unique joy. You may have friends who are older or friends who are younger, friends in a similar life stage and friends in totally different circumstances. Just because you are single in this season of life doesn't mean you can't create a community comprised of other singles, married couples, and growing or already established families. While maintaining friendships with those who are married and have families looks different, your time spent with those in different seasons than you will enrich your life in the here and now. If we open our hearts as single women to learn from those who are married and have families and to spend time at a different pace, we can create a life-giving community that is unique, enjoyable, and all our own.

As a single woman, your most intentional friendships will likely be with those who are married and have kids. You will probably have to be the one who initiates most of your time together because their priorities are different than yours. This doesn't mean they don't want to spend time with you. Don't feel bad if you have to initiate and if you often go to their house as opposed to hosting them at yours. Married couples and families just live at a different pace of life, plain and simple. And it can be so refreshing and de-stressing to spend time in the beautiful chaos of a family movie night, a dinner out at a restaurant, or an afternoon at the park. Once you open yourself up to finding a distinctive community filled with singles, married couples, and families, you will find yourself sharpened and livened by your time spent with all types of friends. It won't be perfect, it might be messy, and it could involve some tantrums, but it will be life-giving. As a single woman, don't limit yourself to friendships with those in a like season, for there is joy to be found in friendship with families.

RIGHT NOW REMINDER:

When your community is comprised of people of different ages and stages, you will learn, grow, and enjoy many different experiences.

ON FRIENDSHIP
WITH SINGLES

So encourage each other and build each other up, just as you are already doing.
I THESSALONIANS 5:11 NLT

No one understands what you're going through better than other single people. From laughing off bad dating stories over lattes, to offering one another advice when you're making tough decisions, to celebrating the wins of an independent single life, a community of single friends is uniquely life-giving and fun. And sometimes it feels like fellow singles just get it. They get what a rollercoaster ride it can be—discouraging, empowering, hopeful, and indifferent. When you are feeling contented in your singleness, other single friends are there to live life with you, go on vacation with you, and be your concert buddy. When you feel confused about your next direction, wondering if you want to start dating or what you should be looking for, other single friends can offer helpful insight and encouragement because they are in it too. And when you are sad or discouraged in your singleness, other single friends can be a shoulder to cry on or a listening ear as you vent.

Friends that are married and have families are really important, but it can be difficult for them to understand the unique challenges and joys of singlehood, especially if they haven't been single for a while. They can lose the insight of the distinctive experience that is being a single person today. As today's verse says, establishing core friendships with other singles offers your heart encouragement and insight so that you may both be built up as well as build others up. Even if your experience of singleness differs from that of your single friends, we've all gone through the ups and downs of this season. Balancing a community that is comprised of singles and those who are married with families will allow for you to feel understood, valued, and a part of a chosen community. And if you are looking to grow your friendships, ask God to provide opportunities and watch Him fill your life.

RIGHT NOW REMINDER:

When your community includes
fellow single people,
you will feel understood,
recognized, and supported.

THE GOOD NEWS IS FOR YOU

This is how God loved the world:
He gave His one and only Son, so that
everyone who believes in Him will not perish
but have eternal life. God sent his Son
into the world not to judge the world,
but to save the world through Him.
JOHN 3:16–17 NLT

We walk around day to day carrying all sorts of burdens and listening to all kinds of lies that we were not meant to shoulder. We think we aren't good enough; we may not be worthy; we can't be loved. But the Good News shows us another way, a life with Christ at the center that is full of joy, peace, and hope. Because of God's immense and unfathomable love for us, He sent Christ to earth to die for us. He did this so that we could have a relationship with Him. And because of Christ's death, our sin and our wrongdoings no longer get in the way of our connection with God. Christ took our mistakes, our failures, and our regrets on Himself and died for them on the cross. And now we are free.

God desires to have a relationship with you

because He loves you more than you can imagine. You were created by Him and will find abundant life in Him. You are never too broken, too lost, or too complicated for God. The Good News of Jesus is for you, and if you don't have a personal relationship with Jesus, today could be your day. Whether we are single, married, separated, divorced, or widowed, we need Jesus. We will find rest in His plan and peace in His presence as we study the Bible and pray to Him and discover His character. We will only find true peace and contentment in our seasons of singleness when we find ourselves rooted in the Good News of the gospel of Jesus Christ.

RIGHT NOW REMINDER:

The gospel is good news because it opens us up to a deep and lasting relationship with Jesus. This Good News is for you today.

LIVE YOUR FAITH

Dear Friend,

This book was prayerfully crafted with you, the reader, in mind. Every word, every sentence, every page was thoughtfully written, designed, and packaged to encourage you—right where you are this very moment. At DaySpring, our vision is to see every person experience the life-changing message of God's love. So, as we worked through rough drafts, design changes, edits, and details, we prayed for you to deeply experience His unfailing love, indescribable peace, and pure joy. It is our sincere hope that through these Truth-filled pages your heart will be blessed, knowing that God cares about you—your desires and disappointments, your challenges and dreams.

He knows. He cares. He loves you unconditionally.

BLESSINGS!
THE DAYSPRING BOOK TEAM

————————